R. note in Back

MW01120632

Criminal Justice
Recent Scholarship

Edited by
Marilyn McShane and Frank P. Williams III

A Series from LFB Scholarly

Tracking the Development of Delinquency

Jessica M. Saunders

LFB Scholarly Publishing LLC
El Paso 2009

Library of Congress Cataloging-in-Publication Data

Saunders, Jessica M., 1978-
 Tracking the development of delinquency / Jessica M. Saunders.
   p. cm. -- (Criminal justice : recent scholarship)
 Includes bibliographical references and index.
 ISBN 978-1-59332-321-9 (alk. paper)
 1. Juvenile delinquency. I. Title.
   HV9069.S28 2009
   364.36--dc22

  2008052588

ISBN 978-1-59332-321-9

Printed on acid-free 250-year-life paper.

Manufactured in the United States of America.

Table of Contents

Tables

Figures

Acknowledgements

Many people significantly contributed to the completion of this work who can not be thanked enough. I would like to recognize a few people in particular who were exceptionally generous with their guidance and expertise. I would above all like to acknowledge Dr. Michael White for his continuance support and encouragement. Additionally, Drs. Josh Freilich, James Lynch, and Keith Marcus provided outstanding assistance and direction. I am also extremely appreciative of the generosity and advice I received from the faculty and staff at The Johns Hopkins Center for Prevention and Early Intervention.

CHAPTER 1.

Introduction

There is an undisputed relationship between age and crime. When crime rates are analyzed by age, offending rates increase through adolescence, peak around 16 or 17 years old, and then drop sharply through the course of young adulthood (Blumstein, Cohen, & Farrington, 1988). The cause of this pattern of antisocial behavior has been the focus of heated debate between criminologists. Traditionally, criminologists have studied the differences between those who engage in crime and those who do not and accepted that differential involvement in criminal activity explains the age-crime curve. Taking an alternative approach, developmental criminologists assume a dynamic approach and focus instead on the development of delinquent behavior over time within individuals. Therefore, developmental theories of crime focus on criminal involvement over various life stages while general theories of crime focus on criminals verses noncriminals. According to developmental theorists, one factor may relate to early offending whereas other factors could cause offending in adolescence, and an entirely different set of factors could be the cause of desistence from criminal behavior in adulthood.

Of course there is heavy debate even within developmental theories. There is an ongoing dispute about what causes the differential involvement in crime over the life-course. Sampson and Laub are on one side of the debate with their fundamental argument that offending patterns within an individual can be meaningfully understood from a revised age-graded theory of informal social control (2005a). Terrie Moffitt, on the other hand, theorized that differential offending patterns can be explained by underlying differences in offender types and not a difference in experiences of informal social control. She put forth the idea that there are distinct groups of offenders, each with its own set of etiologies that have different developmental trajectories of offending (Moffitt, 1993). Each side of the debate has been empirically tested and there are research studies that offer support for both sides. However, it still remains unclear if there are meaningful groups of offender types that have different developmental trajectories of offending or if differences in informal social control are dictating involvement in crime.

The leading developmental theories advanced in the past twenty years is Terrie Moffitt's developmental taxonomy of delinquency, which hypothesized that there are two types of offenders (Moffitt, 1991). The most striking difference between the types of offenders is their continuity and discontinuity of antisocial behavior across age and environment. *Life-course-persistent offenders* begin their antisocial behavior at a young age and continue to offend over their lives. *Adolescence-limited* offenders are involved in criminal behavior only during their adolescent years. The two types of offenders have very different developmental trajectories and causal factors. Life-course-persistent offenders begin manifesting antisocial behavior in infancy or childhood and their etiology lies somewhere in a confluence of psycho-physiological and environmental dysfunction. Adolescence-limited offenders, on the other hand, begin their deviant behavior in adolescence due to a perceived disconnect between their biological and social maturity stages, called the maturity gap. They learn antisocial behavior from their peers and their deviant behavior is reinforced by social rewards. The deviant behavior desists when the rewards no longer outweigh the benefits.

Moffitt's theory is based on this assumption that there are qualitative different types of delinquents and the course of delinquent behavior over time differs between these groups. Therefore, in order to truly explore and test Moffitt's theories, it must be established that there are real group differences in developmental trajectories in delinquent behavior.

The abstainers should have little to no delinquent behavior over time. The adolescent-limited group should increase in their delinquency in adolescence and decrease as they enter adulthood. And finally, Moffitt's taxonomy hypothesizes that the life-course-persistent offenders should display higher rates of delinquency starting at a young age and continuing through adulthood, see the Figure 1, The Theoretical Growth Curve Trajectories on the next page. She also hypothesized that the life-course-persistent offending and abstaining patterns are relatively rare and largest proportion of the population following the adolescence-limited offending pattern.

Moffitt's theory did not simply define distinct groups of delinquents; she also coupled the classifications with hypothesis about their causal factors. She posited that life-course-persistent offenders had very different backgrounds than adolescence-limited offenders, and both of those groups differ from abstainers on several key variables. More specifically, life-course-persistent offenders experienced both psycho-physiological and environmental dysfunctions, which together negatively influence their development. Moffitt hypothesized that there are several mechanisms through which these impact delinquency: (1) psycho-physiological dysfunction, such as attention deficit disorder, conduct disorder, or neurological impairments, which make it more difficult for a child to learn and conform to positive social norms; (2) children who experience environmental dysfunction lack positive role models and support to conform to positive social norms; and, (3) the confluence of "nature" and "nurture" factors make it almost impossible for a child to learn positive behavior early in his/her development which limits his/her response repertoire in later life.

Figure 1. Theoretical Growth Curve Trajectories

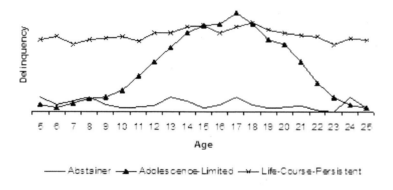

Adolescence-limited offenders are influenced by a very different set of factors. Adolescence is already marked by dramatic changes in aspects of individual development – biological, cognitive, and emotional – that may have relevance for behavioral change. In addition to these individual changes, there are major contextual changes that influence behavior. Like the life-course-persistent offenders, adolescence-limited offenders are influenced by a combination of individual-level factors and contextual factors. According to Moffitt, the important individual-level variable that determines adolescence-limited delinquency is a dissonance between biological and social maturity, what she terms the "maturity gap". This group strives to gain social maturity through engaging in delinquent behavior to match their biological maturity. They learn and mimic this behavior from negative peer role models (from other adolescence-limited and life-course-persistent offenders). The exposure to this delinquent behavior is what Moffitt considers a contextual factor. Adolescence-limited offenders desist in antisocial behavior once the behavior is not rewarding, and thus they can return to the more rewarding prosocial behavior they learned as children.

Moffitt's taxonomy offered fewer concrete hypotheses about what is related to abstaining from delinquency, as do many other criminological theories. Her theory focused on the causes of antisocial behavior, rather than the causes and correlates of prosocial behavior. Her explanation of why some individuals do not become involved in delinquent behavior was that they lacked delinquent role models, or did not experience the maturity gap due to either early social maturity or late biological maturity.

These theories suggest specific causal pathways leading to the different delinquency trajectories, and individual- and contextual-level predictors should predict the different types of offenders. Currently, Moffitt's theories about the causes of delinquency patterns (including abstinence from delinquency) have some empirical support, but are rarely specifically examined in conjunction with group-based trajectory modeling.

The study of patterns of criminal offending and desistence are a central matter of criminological theory and public policy. Presently, there is debate in the field as to whether or not there are distinct subgroups of offenders that follow different trajectories. According to developmental theorists like Terrie Moffitt, there are meaningful groups, and these groups can be distinguished by the manifestation of their offending trajectories and psycho-physiological and environmental differences in their backgrounds, and peer groups and peer models in adolescence. Other theorists like Sampson and Laub do not believe that the offender groups represent any meaningful differences in offending behavior because virtually everyone follows the same pattern.

Thus, the primary research questions of this book will involve the development of antisocial behavior over time and whether there are different subgroups of offenders that can be defined by their developmental trajectories. Taking it one step further, groups with different developmental trajectories can be uncovered, are there differences in their background characteristics, as Moffitt suggested?

This book empirically tests Moffitt's developmental taxonomy of delinquency using a relatively new methodological and statistical technique to model group-based trajectories of delinquency over time. This fairly new technique has been used in over 80 empirical studies since 1994 (Piquero, 2008). Data from the Johns Hopkins Prevention Intervention Research Center's (JHU PIRC) classroom-based, universal preventive intervention trials which were fielded in 1993 in 9 Baltimore City schools is used to examine the developmental trajectories that are central to Moffitt's theory.

This book advances the current understanding of group-based developmental trajectory modeling of delinquency in several ways. It provides an additional study using the group-based modeling of trajectories on an epidemiologically-defined sample youth in Baltimore, Maryland. Many of the previous studies were performed on convenience samples, but this sample is unique in that it captures an entire high-risk urban area. This is important because majority of the empirical studies of group-based trajectories have been performed on a limited number of data sets. Currently, there have been studies on three data sets of offender populations, three data sets with children and adolescence, and between five and ten data sets that have follow-ups into adulthood in the mainstream criminology research literature. This book tests the theory using an entirely different population.

Additionally, this study will take the research one step farther by examining Moffitt's predictions about the different factors associated with offender types. Thus far, few studies have used predictors to explain group membership in the same model that predicts group membership. In other words, some researchers have advanced our understanding of the predictors of group membership by separating subjects into trajectory groups and then running post-hoc analyses of group differences, but this study will actually include the predictors in the same model that predicts group membership, and thus will be less susceptible to misspecification and Type I errors.

In addition, due to the richness of the dataset, Moffitt's specific hypotheses about the differences in the characteristics of the different offender groups are empirically tested. There are measures of the subjects' psycho-physiological deviance, deviant peer groups and peer models, and family dysfunction in the dataset. These predictors will be are added to the model to determine whether her hypotheses about the etiology of developmental trajectories hold empirically. If her theory is supported, it will help identify risk factors for the different developmental trajectories of delinquency that could be used to develop appropriate prevention and intervention programs.

And finally, over and above testing Moffitt's specific theory of trajectories and their etiologies, this book advances the current understanding of group-based trajectories in several ways. It explores the different latent variance structures of the latent growth terms, how they impact group means and variances, class proportions, and group membership. These different variance structures change the meaning of a group, and the implications of these variance structures are discussed. And finally, the way in which predictors are added into the model will be varied in order to test whether they predict group membership or within class variation.

CHAPTER 2.

Moffitt's Taxonomy

One of the few undisputed findings in the study of criminal behavior is the relationship between age and crime. Almost without fail, when official crime rates are analyzed by age, offending incidence increases through adolescence with a peak around 16 or 17 years old, and then drops sharply in young adulthood (Blumstein, Cohen, & Farrington, 1988). Of course, studies of arrests and convictions identify only a small fraction of criminal activity, as most of it remains undetected by officials. However there is strong evidence, using both official and unofficial measures of crime, that the majority of offenders are teenagers. By the early 20s, the number of offenders drops by around 50%, with 85% of offenders desisting from criminal involvement by 28, see Figure 2, The Aggregate Age-Crime Curve on the next page (Blumstein & Cohen, 1987; Farrington, 1986).

The traditional age-crime curve begins around age 10 because the left side is censored due to lack of official data on children and crime. Many researchers have extended the curve into childhood by including antisocial behaviors that manifest in childhood, and sometimes as far back as infancy (Loeber, Stouthamer-Loeber, Van Kammen, & Farrington, 1989; Moffitt, 1990). Evidence of the validity and reliability of this trend has been found using different samples in cross-cultural and cross-temporal research. In recent historical periods for which there is reliable data, the age-crime trend is virtually identical to the one pictured above. This relationship has also been found in several different Western countries and in both males and females (Hirschi & Gottfredson, 1985).

Theories to explain the age-crime curve and juvenile delinquency can be divided into two main categories: static and developmental. The first group of theories look for the causes of delinquency in a cross sectional fashion; that is, the causes of crime work in the same manner at each developmental stage. These theories are very appealing because they point to a few causes of antisocial behavior and give great insight and simplicity in developing crime prevention strategies.

Most theories of crime and delinquency seek to determine the cause of antisocial behavior in biological, psychological, or social factors, and are based on the assumption that these processes operate identically regardless of age. General theorists, or those that believe in a static explanation of crime, propose that age is unnecessary to understand antisocial behavior (Bartusch, Lynam, Moffitt, & Silva, 1997). However, many developmental theorists believe that these explanations are too simplistic in their views of deviance and human development. Therefore, in contrast to these theories, developmental theories consider different factors influencing antisocial behavior at different ages.

Figure 2. The Aggregate Age-Crime Curve[1]

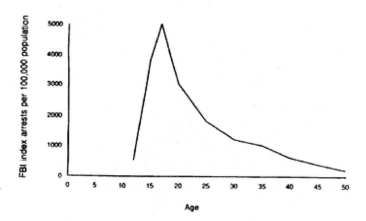

A large number of studies focus on the differences between offenders and nonoffenders; however, developmental and life-course researchers approach the study of crime from a different perspective and focus instead on the importance of distinguishing the developmental course of offending within the offender population (Moffitt, 1993; Loeber, 1982; Sampson and Laub, 1992). This research has uncovered diverse trajectories of offending, which emphasizes the importance of phases of the offending cycle from onset to desistence.

---

[1] Age-specific arrest rates for United States Federal Bureau of Investigation's (FBI) index offenses in 1980. (Index offenses include homicide, forcible rape, robbery, aggravated assault, burglary, larceny, and auto theft. From "Criminal Career Research: Its Value for Criminology" by A. Blumstein, J.Cohen, and D.P. Farrington, 1988. *Criminology, 26,* p.11.

Differential offending trajectories have been replicated in multiple longitudinal studies on criminal behavior, during different time periods, and in different parts of the world. Studies on criminal behavior in the United States, Canada, Puerto Rico, England, Scotland, Denmark, Sweden, Finland, China, Japan, Switzerland, Australia, New Zealand, all of which employ different sampling frames and data analysis techniques, support this conclusion (e.g., Broidy et al., 2003; Weitekams and Kerner, 1994).

According to developmental theorists, one factor may relate to childhood offending whereas a different factor could cause offending through adolescence, and an entirely different set of factors could be the cause of desistence from criminal behavior. They maintain that as people mature and enter different stages of their lives, different social, cultural, and developmental forces are influencing their behavior in different ways. For example, during childhood, family characteristic effects are much stronger than in adolescence, when peer effects become dominant in explaining delinquent behavior.

There are two main factions in developmental theories, those that track criminal propensity and those that track career criminals. Gottfredson and Hirschi (1990) are the leaders on the criminal propensity side; they theorize that some people are more prone to commit crimes, but this inclination remains consistent throughout their lifetimes. Gottfredson and Hirschi claim that self-control, which is established by 8-10 years of age, predicts crime such that external life events no longer exert as strong an effect.[2] The changes in criminal involvement over the life course do not reflect different propensities because everyone follows the same age-crime curve. According to this theory, the only variables that need to be explained are those that determine an individual's criminal propensity in their youth. This type of research can be accomplished using cross-sectional research and does not require the more expensive and difficult longitudinal research methodologies.

The other side of developmental theories tracks criminal careers, examining the possibility that the same sets of variables may not be responsible for criminal involvement during different points over the life course. With this framework, it is necessary to build different

---

[2] While Gottfredson and Hirschi believe that self-control is unmalleable after childhood, differential offending rates over the life course can be explained by different opportunities to commit crimes.

models for age of onset, participation, frequency, duration, and desistence of criminal behavior. In essence, the debate is whether there is one set of factors that is associated with criminal involvement and this does not vary with age, or if there are different sets of variables that work at different developmental stages that are associated with, or causal factors of, criminal involvement.

Sampson and Laub claim that changes in informal social control (such as marriage and military experience) can alter criminal trajectories. They emphasize an age-graded theory of informal social control, where important life domains at different points in time influence behavior differentially (Sampson & Laub, 2005a). Other developmental theorists, like Patterson, Moffitt, and Loeber, posit that trajectories can be influenced by a mixture of static, dynamic, and developmental processes, such that offenders differ on offending rates due to a confluence of factors on multiple levels. The developmental taxonomic theories focus on categories of offenders, identifying at least two types of offenders – early onset persisters and late-onset desisters (Moffitt, 1993; Patterson, 1996). Terrie Moffitt (1993) has advanced a developmental dual taxonomy of delinquency. According to Moffitt's theory, the age-crime curve disguises two criminal trajectories because of its reliance on aggregate data. According to her theory, there are two different types of offenders: the life-course-persistent offender and the adolescent-limited offender.

MOFFITT'S DEVELOPMENTAL PERSPECTIVE

Terrie Moffitt proposed a dual taxonomy of offenders in 1993 that was innovative, not only because of its predictions about developmental trajectories of offending, but because it put forth the idea that there are distinct developmental clusters of trajectories of antisocial behavior that are the result of divergent etiologies. The most striking difference between the offender types is their continuity and discontinuity of antisocial behavior across age and environmental context. Life-course-persistent offenders begin their antisocial behavior at a young age and continue to display these characteristics over their lives, whereas adolescence-limited offenders are involved in criminal behavior only through their adolescent years. The two types of offenders have very different developmental trajectories and causal factors. Life-course-persistent offenders begin manifesting antisocial behavior in infancy or childhood, and their etiology lies in a confluence of psycho-physiological and environmental deviance. Adolescence-limited offenders begin their deviant behavior in adolescence due to a perceived disconnect between their biological and social maturity stages. They are exposed to antisocial behavior by their peers and it is reinforced by coveted social rewards. Adolescence-limited offenders desist from criminal involvement when the rewards no longer outweigh the benefits, as they are rational thinkers. Inherent in this theory is that there is one other group, those who abstain from any involvement in criminal behavior.

Life-Course-Persistent Offenders

According to Moffitt's developmental theory (1993), a life-course-persistent offender (LCP) is a statistically aberrant type of offender whose antisocial behavior remains consistent over his/her life and across multiple domains. The LCP offender begins displaying antisocial behavior in infancy or as a young child, and continues to display deviant behavior throughout his/her life.

Life-course-persistent offenders begin their antisocial careers as early as infancy, where it is manifested through measures of antisocial behavior and official diagnoses of conduct disorder. With these offenders, there appears to be persistent stability in antisocial behavior across time and diverse circumstances. According to Moffitt, (1997: 13):

> "[t]he topography of their behavior may change due to changing opportunities, but the disposition to act antisocially persists throughout the life course. The professional nomenclature may change, but the faces remain the same as they drift through successive systems aimed at curbing their deviance; schools, juvenile-justice programs, psychiatric treatment centers, and prisons."

What causes someone to become a life-course-persistent offender? This question has only begun to be explored in the research literature. According to Moffitt, it is associated with early neurological impairment and early risk factors during pre-birth or infancy. Research tends to support this position as it has been found that people displaying extreme antisocial behavior from ages 3 to 15 have histories of conduct disorder and ADHD, as well as other neuropsychological dysfunction, along with poor verbal skills and executive functions. Longitudinal studies conducted in New Zealand and Pittsburgh found that neurological dysfunction in conjunction with early childhood displays of aggressive antisocial behavior were associated with persistence in negative behavioral patterns (Moffitt, 1993).

Moffitt's theory does not take a biologically deterministic stance. Although there is evidence that anatomical structures and physiological processes within the nervous system influence antisocial behavior, these processes can also be caused by social and/or environmental variables. In support of her theory, social and structural aspects of the environment have been linked to neuropsychological impairments. Moffitt argues that biological determinants of psychological characteristics co-occur with family disadvantage and deviance, and therefore it is difficult, if not impossible, to disentangle the effects. In her theory, biological origins are not deterministic, but rather set the stage for subsequent person-environment interactions. Currently, it is unknown if these early behavioral difficulties contribute to the development of persistent antisocial behavior by evoking responses from interpersonal social environment which exacerbate the child's tendencies. However, according to Moffitt (1993: 682):

> "it is immaterial whether parent-child similarities arise from shared genes or shared homes. A home environment wherein prenatal care is haphazard, drugs are used during pregnancy, and infants' nutritional needs are neglected is a setting where sources of children's neuropsychological dysfunction that are clearly environmental coexist with a criminogenic social environment."

It is possible that this dysfunctional interaction style is the mechanism through which the negative behavior is maintained through the life course. Evidence suggests that life-course-persistent antisocial children are ignored and rejected by other children because of their unpredictable, aggressive behavior; however, they enjoy the benefits of social maturity that others do not. The life-course-persistent offender reaches social maturity at an earlier age because of his rule-violating behavior and becomes perceived in a favorable manner by his age mates. Although his age mates might admire him for achieving a higher status in society, they do not necessarily befriend the life-course-persistent offender because of his erratic, impulsive, and sometimes violent behavior.

Why does the life-course-persistent offender continue to commit crime through his/her life? According to Moffit, they never learned how to behave in a socially acceptable manner because of their backgrounds containing personality disorders, cognitive deficits, and dysfunctional environments. Since they never experienced proper socialization, they are unable to respond to the changing rewards and punishments throughout their lifetimes, and continue on their antisocial paths.

Adolescence-Limited Offenders

The adolescence-limited offenders only display antisocial and criminal behavior during adolescence and desist from this behavior in their 20s. Adolescence-limited offending appears to be ubiquitous, with the majority of adolescents joining this group for at least a short period before desisting from crime. In fact, in one study only 7% of a sample of 18-year olds denied being involved in any delinquent activities in the previous year (Moffitt, 1991). Moffitt hypothesized that adolescence-limited offending occurs in both males and females as long as the two conditions are met: (1) access to antisocial models and (2) perceived consequences of delinquency are positive and rewarding. These adolescents mimic the life-course-persistent offenders in order to gain social status in a time of transition, which she calls the "maturity gap".

The maturity gap stems from a disconnect between biological and social maturity, which has changed dramatically over the past hundred years. Modernization has led to earlier biological maturity and an even larger delay in social maturity. Fifty years ago, an individual would reach social maturity around 18 years old; but today, social maturity and economic self-sufficiency are delayed and not realized until later in life (Nebesio & Pescoritz, 2005). When an adolescent reaches physical adulthood (e.g. sexual maturity), there are still many years before he or she reaches social adulthood, and many adolescents fight for some social recognition of their adult status through antisocial behavior. Puberty coupled with access to deviant peer role models, who appear to enjoy a highly desirable adult-like social status, is the important determinant of adolescence-onset delinquency according to Moffitt's theory. The adolescence-limited delinquents learn antisocial behavior from their peers and the deviant behavior is reinforced by social rewards and feelings of maturity. Through this process, the antisocial precocity of life-course-persistent offenders becomes a coveted social asset and the adolescence-limited offenders commit crimes to serve their desire for acknowledgement and privilege. Therefore, adolescence-limited offending is a product of an interaction between age, social status, and environment.

Moffitt hypothesized (1993) that while adolescence-onset offenders mimic their life-course-persistent peers, this does not require close friendships; the adolescence-onset offender needs only to observe the perceived social benefits and more adult-like style of their antisocial peers. In the start of adolescence, a few individuals join in antisocial behavior with the life-course-persistent ones, and then a few more, until a critical mass is reached where virtually all adolescents are drawn in to some criminal behavior with their peers. The strong effects of peer influences on antisocial behavior have been consistently found in the research literature and can be interpreted in terms of imitation or vicarious reinforcement, both of which would support Moffitt's theory (e.g., Agnew, 1991; Felson & Hayne, 2002; Herrenkohl et al., 2000).

Because this type of offending is about gaining social status, it can be modified with appropriate rewards and punishments, which should be able to help explain desistence in young adulthood. Since these offenders do not have a lifelong history of antisocial behavior, they are able to recognize and respond to different reinforcements. Adolescence-limited offenders would persist in criminal involvement if they never perceived a change of social rewards, but according to Moffitt, once they reach adulthood, the cost/benefit ratio changes in such a way as to tip the scales against delinquent behavior.

Abstainers

Unfortunately, much less is known about the individuals who abstain completely from antisocial behavior. As criminologists tend to study those who are involved in the criminal justice system and not those who are not, the field is lacking in research regarding individuals who never get involved in crime. Possible explanations offered by Moffitt include the conjecture that some youth may never experience the maturity gap and/or lack antisocial role models, either because of (1) late puberty, (2) early initiation into adult roles, (3) strong resilience characteristics, or (4) limited access to antisocial peers to mimic.

Piquero, Brezina, and Turner (2005) examined some of Moffitt's predictions about those who abstain from delinquent behavior through adolescence using the National Longitudinal Survey of Youth 1997. Using self-report measurements of delinquency, abstainers were defined as youths who had never engaged in thirteen types of antisocial activities. They found that abstainers were more likely to be female, have a lower proportion of delinquent peers, a greater attachment to teachers, a higher degree of parental monitoring, are less physically mature, have lower levels of "sadness/depression", and are less autonomous than their delinquent peers. The most important findings with regard to Moffitt's theory are that lower proportion of delinquent peers and delayed physical maturity are associated with abstention from delinquency. However, contrary to Moffitt's theory, abstainers were not social loners shut out of the delinquent scene as she expected, but instead tended to have more prosocial friends.

Offender Type Distinctions

Two of the most striking differences between the offender types are their continuity and discontinuity of antisocial behavior across age and situation, along with type of crime they commit. Adolescence-limited offenders, since they respond to rewards and punishments, are not antisocial in all situations. Life-course-persistent offenders, on the other hand, remain markedly consistent in their antisocial behavior across both time and situation.

Life-course-persistent offenders makes up a very small proportion of the population. type of offender is more often male than female, with 6% of males fitting this pattern but only 1%-2% of females offending across their lifetimes (Kratzer & Hodgins, 1999). Kratzer and Hodgins also found that 70% of crimes were committed by the six percent of males who began displaying signs of antisocial behavior early in childhood. Other researchers have found that early arrest is the best predictor of long-term recidivism and persistence in a criminal lifestyle through adulthood. Adolescence-limited offenders, on the other hand, are much more plentiful in the population, with Moffitt and others suggesting that it might be statistically anomalous to abstain from crime during adolescence (Elliott et al., 1993; Hirschi, 1969; Moffitt & Silva, 1988). In fact, most police contacts are made during adolescence (Farrington, Ohlion, & Wilson, 1986).

Adolescence-limited offenders are also involved in a different sort
of crime than their life-course-persistent counterparts. They are more
likely to be involved with antisocial acts that assert their social maturity
and reinforce their personal independence, such as curfew violations,
vandalism, public order offences, truancy, theft, automobile theft, early
pregnancy, and alcohol and drug usage, while life-course-persistent
offenders will be engaged in more person-orientated and other violent
offences. Delinquent acts such as tobacco, alcohol, and other drug
abuse are reinforced during adolescence because they symbolize
independence and maturity, not necessarily a predilection toward crime
or violence. However, by age 15, adolescent-limited and life-course-
persistent offenders look alike in the variety of laws broken, frequency
of laws broken, and number of times in court (Moffitt, 1991). They
begin to differ once again once the adolescence-limited offenders begin
desisting from crime after their social maturity catches up with their
biological maturity and the rewards of engaging in delinquent behavior
no longer outweigh the benefits.

LONGITUDINAL STUDIES RESEARCH RELATED TO MOFFITT'S DEVELOPMENTAL TAXONOMY

A relatively new methodology has been developed to examine patterns
of delinquency over time which is uniquely appropriate to test
developmental taxonomies. There have been over 80 studies using
group-based trajectory modeling in the criminological literature
between 1993 and 2004 (Piquero, 2008). These studies have examined
group-based trajectories of various manifestations of antisocial
behavior in urban, suburban, and rural settings in the United States and
abroad, using different time frames from birth through age 70. Over a
dozen group-based trajectory studies have been published using United
States-based general populations, using birth cohorts, high-risk urban
samples, and national databases. There have also been quite a few
international studies using this methodological approach. This
methodology has identified between two and nine groups, with the
majority finding three of four distinct trajectory groups, which suggests
that the findings are reliable. They have generally supported many of
Moffitt's assertions and are described in more detail in the following
sections.

Group-Based Developmental Studies Using Only Offender Populations

Six trajectory studies using three data sets have examined trajectories in offender populations (Boston: Laub, Nagin, & Sampson, 1998, California: Piquero et al, 2001, and Great Brittan: Francis, Soothill, & Fligelstone, 2004). All of the data sets and analyses support the idea that there are several distinct developmental trajectories. The three data sets have found between three and nine distinct offending trajectories; most uncovered between four and six groups, depending on the measurement of criminality, the length of follow-up, and gender (Eggleston et al., 2004; Sampson and Laub, 2003; Piquero, Brame, Mazerolle, & Haapenen, 2002; Francis et al., 2004). Together, their findings also imply that there are between four and six distinct offending trajectories, reliant on observation window and dependent measure. The studies suggest that offending declines as early adulthood regardless of group membership. They do not, however, address questions about what factors are related to the different trajectories within offender populations or examine nonoffenders, who make up the majority of the general population.

Blockland, Nagin, and Nieuwbeerta's (2005) study found four offender trajectories and began to explore the differences between offender types. While some of their findings support Moffitt's theory, others conflicted with her hypotheses. For instance, they found that life-course-persistent offenders were not involved with violent, person-centered crime, but rather this group tended to be drug addicts. Of course, these are examining different types within offender populations and do not include nonoffending populations, which is vital for testing Moffitt's theory.

Group-Based Developmental Studies of Childhood and Adolescence

Several more studies concentrated on the developmental trajectories of aggressive behavior in childhood and their findings demonstrate a great deal of consistency despite using different dependent measures of aggression. Each of the studies supported the idea that there are reliable group-based developmental trajectories. Broidy et al. (2003) found four different physical aggression trajectories in boys between ages 7½ and 10½. Tremblay et al. (2004) found three trajectories in aggression from 17 to 42 month olds. The final study, conducted by Shaw and colleagues (2003) found four trajectories of conduct problems between ages 2 and 8.

The studies that continued to follow subjects into adolescence also reveal a great deal of consistency. Nagin and colleagues (2003) found four trajectories of physical aggression from ages 10 to 15 (low, moderate declining, high declining, and chronic groups). Broidy and colleagues (2003) used six different data sets from three countries to examine the course of physical aggression in childhood (as early as 6) through early adolescence (as late as age 15). They found three or four trajectories across all of the six studies, which vary by gender, follow-up period, and sample. A majority of the studies use dependent measures of externalizing (but not always delinquent) behaviors and a combination of different self-report measures (either by teacher, parent, or self).

Comparable results and conclusions can be drawn from virtually all the studies. Regardless of source of the outcome measure (self-, teacher-, parent-report, or objective antisocial behaviors), analogous substantive conclusions about the shape and number of trajectories can be made. By the end of adolescence, most trajectories are on the decline. Predictably, three to four trajectories are uncovered, which generally follow a low, medium, and high group. However, none of these studies continued into adulthood to test the fundamental theoretical issues with whether these different patterns persist through the lifecourse. The high group roughly fits Moffitt's conceptualization of the life-course-persistent offender, the medium group most closely approximates her adolescence-limited, and the low group resembles the abstainers; however without following the subjects through adulthood it is hard to draw any firm conclusions with regard to Moffitt's theory.

Group-Based Developmental Studies Spanning the Life Course

The majority, and perhaps most theoretically meaningful studies, of group-based trajectory studies have spanned childhood, adolescence, and adulthood (e.g., Bushway, Thornberry, & Krohn, 2003; Chung et al, 2002; D'Unger et al., 1998; 2002; Laub, Nagin, & Sampson, 1998; Paternoster et al., 2001; Piquero, et al., 2002; Sampson & Laub, 2003). These studies span several continents, time periods, and sampling frames. As with the other study sampling frames, there are striking similarities in the findings across these studies.

These studies found that there are different antisocial trajectories and that these share consistency across diverse samples with respect to the number of groups. For the most part, they have used a combination of self-report and official records as dependent measures. Each study found evidence of different groups of developmental trajectories, and the differences in the shapes and number of the trajectories uncovered in these studies appears to be due to different follow-up lengths, dependent measures, and data collection frequency (see Piquero, 2008).

The studies found an adolescence-peaking pattern and a chronic offending pattern, which supports Moffitt's theory. However, they have also found other groups of offenders not identified by her theory, such as a late-onset group, a low-level chronic group, and an intermittent offender group. Another interesting difference between some of the studies is the age at which antisocial behavior peaks – some studies find a peak in adolescence whereas others found the peak in early adulthood.

Despite the considerable differences, there are a number of typical age and group patterns that clearly emerge from the studies. In general, there is a low, high, moderate but declining, and a late onset group. The studies offer limited support of Moffitt's developmental taxonomy: The low rate groups generally appear be similar to Moffitt's abstainers, the high rate group is similar to her hypotheses about the life-course-persistent offenders, and the moderate but declining and late onset groups could be conceptualized as the adolescence-limited offenders, depending on the shape of the trajectories.

Overall, the actual number of groups and their specific trajectories seem to vary by dependent variable, with self-, parent-, and teacher-reports containing higher frequencies of delinquency and more trajectory subgroups than official report data. In addition, the number of groups and shapes of their trajectories are noticeably sensitive to follow-up period, with longer follow-ups revealing more groups with greater slope variation. It is important to note that although there are slightly different findings depending on both the dependent variable and observation window, similar theoretical inferences can be drawn from these studies, which increases both the validity and reliability of the conclusions.

Criticisms of Moffitt's Developmental Taxonomy

Not everyone agrees with Moffitt or interprets the empirical findings as supportive of her hypotheses. Sampson and Laub (2005a) disagree with Moffitt's theory on two main grounds. They found that life-course desistance is the norm everyone, regardless of what age they began offending. This does not necessarily conflict with Moffitt's theory, as she does not make any specific hypotheses to conflict independent age-crime relationship (Moffitt, 1993). For example, she never claims that life-course-persistent offenders continue to offend at a high rate their entire lives, and therefore the possibility of decline in the frequency and/or severity of offending in later life is not necessarily inconsistent with her theory (Nagin & Tremblay, 2005b). However, Sampson and Laub feel that this relationship between crime and age in later years invalidates Moffitt's taxonomy because virtually all offenders eventually desist, even the life-course-persistents. They have written that they would be more supportive of her theory if she relabeled the life-course-persistent offenders as "high rate yet declining with age" they would be more supportive of her theory.

Empirically, there are criticisms of the theory as well. In the over 80 studies of group-based developmental trajectories reviewed by Piquero (2008), none of the studies found a two group model of offending. The exact number of distinct offense trajectories remains a matter of substantial debate, but there is evidence that Moffitt's model may be too simplistic and there is evidence of at least two other offender types. Nagin, Farrington, and Moffitt (1995) found four different trajectories; (1) the never convicted, (2) adolescence-limited, (3) high-level chronics, and (4) low-level chronics. Kratzer and Hodgins (1999) identified five trajectories: (1) early starters, who are approximately 6% of the male population and .5% of the female population, (2) adolescence-limited, which is made up by approximately 10% of the male population and 2% of the female population, (3) adult starters, which is made up of approximately 13% of the male population and 4% of the female population, (4) discontinuous offenders, which is made up of 4% of the male population and .5% of the female population, and (5) abstainers.

Chung and colleagues (2002) also found five groups of offenders based on offending trajectories, which contradicts Moffitt's theory – nonoffenders (24%), late onsetters (14.4%), desisters (35.3%), escalators (19.3%), and chronics (7%). The chronic group was found to be similar to Moffitt's life-course-persistent offenders, and the late onset group shared certain features of adolescence-limited offenders; however, the other groups were not anticipated by her theory. However, their finding of five distinct groups does not hold across all or even that majority of group-based developmental trajectory models. For example, Nagin and Tremblay (1999) did not find evidence of this late onset aggression group using ratings of physically aggressive behavior in childhood; but rather found four groups: (1) low aggression, (2) moderate declining aggression, (3) high declining aggression, and (4) chronic aggressors. In fact, at least six different data sets from around the world have failed to identify a late onset group (Broidy et al., 2003), and the validity of this group of offenders is questionable. Of course, even if this trajectory is highly unusual, it does not rule out the possibility of its existence.

In general there have been two or three unanticipated groups identified through group-based developmental trajectory modeling research: the adult- or late-adolescence starter, the discontinuous (or episodic) offender, and the low-level chronic. The adult-onset type of offender abstains from criminal behavior during childhood and adolescence and does not begin offending until reaching adulthood. This type of offender is extremely unusual, and may commit only non-violent offenses, and is believed to be highly unusual (Brame, Nagin, & Tremblay, 2001; Kratzer & Hodgins, 1999). The discontinuous/ episodic offender commits crime at irregular intervals throughout his/her life. They differ from the life-course-persistent offender in that their antisocial and criminal behavior does not occur frequently, but rather occasionally, and not necessarily across diverse social situations. One final type, the low-level chronic offender, displays low levels of antisocial behavior across their life-course. While these offender types have been uncovered in a few empirical studies, there existence has not been reliably found across studies, and therefore, it is unclear whether they are simply data artifacts or real groups.

CHAPTER 3.

A New Approach

This chapter will provide an overview of the methodology used for this study. To appropriately test Moffitt's developmental taxonomy, a relatively new statistical analysis technique was applied to data to empirically derive developmental trajectories of delinquency. At the same time, this statistical analysis technique was explored, as there are not many specific guidelines about model specification. These model specifications were also systematically tested to evaluate the appropriateness of the technique both empirically and theoretically. The methodology and the rational for selecting this approach are described in detail below.

A conceptual framework that considers the developmental trajectories of offending requires a different analytic strategy from those typically used in cross-sectional criminological research. Instead of focusing on the average association between outcomes and predictors for all study participants, a method that can classify individuals into sub-groups based on their offense trajectories is important for testing developmental taxonomies. In relation to antisocial development and criminology, many different models consistent with an approach of this kind have been employed in the past. Some use variants of cluster analytic techniques to identify homogenous sub-groups of individuals based on characteristics assessed at different times during different developmental periods, while others used more ad-hoc approaches. Luckily, recent methodological, statistical, and technological advances have made a new approach possible that can more appropriately test Moffitt's theory.

According to Piquero (2008), the testing of Moffitt's developmental taxonomy could not be accomplished using the widely accepted single-group frameworks advanced by other life-course theorists like Gottfredson and Hirschi or Sampson and Laub. Statistical techniques to test group-based longitudinal theories must have the ability to parcel distinct offending trajectories that change in shape and level over time. Methodologies, such as hierarchical modeling and latent growth modeling have been used to test developmental theories for decades; however, they are not appropriate to test this theory because they treat the population distribution of the development of criminal activity as continuous, whereas Moffitt's theory of trajectory groups approximates a latent multinomial distribution.

Group-based trajectory modeling is an application of finite mixture modeling and an elaboration of conventional maximum likelihood models (Muthen 2004; Nagin, 2005; Nagin & Tremblay, 2005b). This relatively new methodological and statistical technique is needed because it can go beyond identifying averages and variability, to uncover possible distinctive trajectories within the population. The group-based approach is a systematic way of categorizing offenders by discerning different groups using formal and objective statistical criterion (Nagin, 2005; Nagin & Tremblay, 2004). This method is uniquely suited for testing taxonomic dimensions of offending trajectories (Piquero, 2008). Using the parametric, semi-parametric, or mixed Poisson model options (depending on type of dependent variable), each individual has a probability of belonging to each group and can be assigned to the group to which s/he has the highest probability. The most important scientific question related to this methodology is whether these latent groups make better predictions of future behavior. This question has yet to be answered.

Group-based trajectory analysis techniques have been developed to model meaningful sub-groups within a population that follow a distinctive developmental trajectory (Nagin & Land, 1993; Nagin, 2005). This relatively new modeling technique does not make parametric assumptions about the unobserved heterogeneity distribution in the population and the mixing distribution is viewed as multinomial. Each category in the multinomial mixture can be viewed as a meaningful grouping for the unobserved distribution of individual heterogeneity.

An important subject that has been generally overlooked in the studies of developmental taxonomies is in the empirical and theoretical definition of a group. Almost all of the studies employ an estimation technique that defines group in a very narrow manner: a group of people that follow an identical developmental pathway where only random error accounts for each individual's deviation from their group average. Regardless of the manner in which the model is defined, group members will never follow their trajectory groups perfectly (Nagin, 2005; Nagin & Tremblay, 2005a; 2005b), but the question of modeling within group heterogeneity has only begun to be addressed and has never been specifically discussed in conjunction with any developmental theory (Kreuter & Muthén, 2007; 2008). Kreuter and Muthén (2008) demonstrate the utility of applying the different modeling techniques that incorporate within group variation using criminological data, but acknowledge that ultimately model selection should rely on substantive theory. Unfortunately, theory is particularly lacking in this area.

How would one go about making modeling decisions based on a theory? Again, there is very little guidance provided by theorists at this point, even from a well developed theory such as Moffitt's. Her theory does not explicitly address the question of within-group variation, although it can be argued that the modeling decisions are implicit in some of her hypotheses.

First, her abstainer (AB) group is assumed to never engage in delinquent or antisocial behavior regardless of age or environmental context. Implicit in that hypothesis is that this group would be homogeneous in their displays of no delinquency. The adolescence-limited (AL) group, on the other hand, displays antisocial and delinquent behavior due to their experience of the "maturity gap" and exposure to delinquent peer role models. Their displays of delinquent behavior peak in adolescence because this is when they experience the largest "gap" between physical and social maturity. They might not display antisocial behavior across all situations because they are environmentally motivated and use crime as a means to gain social status. Each individual in this group would have a unique experience with the maturity gap because there is variation that ages at which physical and social maturity occur. There would also be more variability in the situations in which delinquent behavior was observed, as they display deviant behavior in different situations in order to gain social approval. In addition, they would vary in their exposure to delinquent peers. The implications for modeling would be that there would be a substantial amount of trajectory heterogeneity within this group.

The life-course-persistent (LCP) group is hypothesized to begin their antisocial behavior at a young age and continue to display these characteristics over their life course. These individuals should also display antisocial behavior and across environment and situation due to a convergence of ecological and psycho-physiological difficulties. Moffitt does not specify the absolute level of delinquency that should be observed at any period, except that it remains "high", and it is not clear how high their levels should be, especially when considering different manifestations of antisocial behavior. In terms of modeling implications, the LCP group should be identified regardless of outcome measurement and follow up period. As for the heterogeneity of the group, it is less clear as to whether this group would be homogenous; for instance, could and LCP offender display antisocial behavior at lower levels throughout his/her life course? Could there also be an age graded process such that they decline over time but still exhibit antisocial behavior? It is conceptually unclear how much variation would be expected in the LCP trajectory group.

Presently there are two main statistical software programs that can estimate group-based trajectory models. One is a SAS-based procedure called Proc Traj, available through the National Consortium of Violence Research at *www.ncovr.org* (Jones and Nagin, 2005; Jones, Nagin, & Roeder, 2001). The second is using a generalized growth mixture modeling program (GGMM), MPlus, developed by Muthén and colleagues (Muthén, 1989; Muthén & Muthén 1998- 2004). GGMM allows variation around the group means and slopes, and is therefore more flexible and able to capture the population with fewer latent classes (Bauer & Curran 2003; 2004). MPlus also allows for simultaneous modeling of different groups and would allow the control, classroom centered intervention, and family-school partnership conditions models to be estimated at the same time if necessary.

There are several limitations to this methodology which must be acknowledged. Group-based trajectory methodology is limited because it aims to summarize behavior and characteristics of individuals following similar developmental courses and individuals in each group will not necessarily follow the overall trajectory (or even their own group) flawlessly (Nagin, 2005; Nagin & Tremblay, 2005a; 2005b). In fact, the groupings within the trajectory is simply a cluster of approximately homogenous individuals in the sense that they are following approximately the same developmental course which has distinctive characteristics from other clusters of individuals following different developmental courses. This method assumes that the underlying distribution is drawn from a multinomial (discrete) population, and there will be model misspecification if that unobserved heterogeneity is actually drawn from a continuous distribution (Piquero, 2008; Raudenbush, 2005). In addition to this problem, the classification of individuals into groups will never be perfect and the number of groups extracted is variable and sensitive to sample size

(Nagin, 2005). However, the number of groups appears to stabilize around a sample size of 500 (D'Unger et al., 1998).

Perhaps the greatest pitfall associated with this methodology lies within its interpretation. This method is vulnerable to misinterpretation by those pre-disposed to the idea of high-rate offenders. According to Sampson et al. (2004:41), the greatest pitfall is that it:

"begins with the assumption that groups exist, often leading to the notion that a wide array of group configurations is possible. Is it then easy for the naïve user to conclude (tautologically?) that groups exist because they are discovered, even though a model cannot be said to discover what it assumes."

Bauer and Curran found the same pitfalls with the methodology (2003: 358):

"[t]his approach reverses the normal hypothestico-deductive process of science. Specifically, using a growth mixture model to test the hypothesis that the population is heterogeneous and then proceeding to interpret the latent classes as true subgroups because that is what theory suggests would be affirming the consequence."

It is therefore important to remember that regardless of how groups are defined, they are only an approximation of a more complex unobserved reality (Nagin & Tremblay, 2005a; 2005b). One must interpret the results of the groupings with caution, as the groupings are only approximations of population differences in developmental trajectories. Using this methodology to demonize a group is not helpful, whereas, using this methodology to identify risk characteristics within specific trajectories could have vast implications for prevention and intervention research (Nagin & Tremblay, 2005a; 2005b).

According to Raudenbush (2005), the modeling approach is retrospective and data-driven instead of theory-driven, and therefore the groups could be simply data artifacts. However, over fifty studies using this methodology have found strikingly similar and reliable patterns, and it is unlikely that the groupings are data artifacts. Simulation studies have found that this technique would produce empirically superior results than a single-group growth process even if the true population is homogenous (Bauer & Curran, 2003), which is problematic and must be further examined.

As there are still many questions about the reliability and validity of group-based trajectory models, this study also examined the many models need to be estimated to successively test different model specifications that correspond to the different combinations of group heterogeneity.

The initial model estimated is pictured in Figure 3 with the intercept, time and time-squared variables residuals set to zero to mimic the SAS approach and limit within-group variability. The error variances in the first and second data collection period will be allowed to covary because they are both collected from the same teacher (in the Fall and Spring of first grade). The model was then re-estimated with each combinations of the parameters freed to test the model constraints. According to Bauer & Curran (2003) the growth factor functional forms are often held invariant not for theoretical reasons, but for statistical expediency. This study systematically freed and fixed the different model constraints by fixing parameters and their variation to be invariant over group. The theoretical and methodological meanings of the different models is explored and discussed as the findings apply to Moffitt's theory in the following chapters.

Figure 3. *Initial Estimation Model*

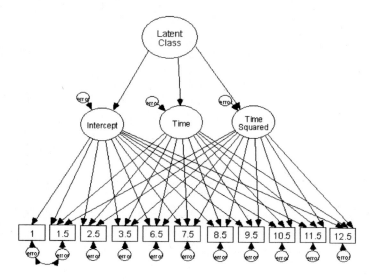

According to Moffitt's developmental taxonomy, this model should be sufficient because there are the only three classes of offenders including the abstainers; however, it should be noted that there is evidence of additional types in the research literature. While the more parameter values that can be set a priori, the more theory driven the test becomes, these assumptions also need to be checked empirically. Therefore, additional patterns of offending were investigated, such as low-level persistents, childhood-limited, and episodic offenders. The model was re-estimated using different numbers of latent classes (developmental trajectories) and different proportions of subjects in each latent class to find the optimal model to fit the data.

After the groups were defined, each group's developmental trajectory of offending was examined. The number of groups as well as their shapes was analyzed and interpreted with respect to Moffitt's hypotheses. The theoretical meaning of the different group trajectories and how they support or refute Moffitt's theory is discussed in the following chapters.

The differences between the groups were also explored. Moffitt's theory dictated the direction of these analyses. The dataset provided a wealth of variables that can test each of Moffitt's hypotheses and data reduction techniques were performed to utilize all available information. Variables from the parent, teacher, and self-report surveys were combined to explore the effects of different life domains (e.g., family, school, peer, and individual) at different developmental periods, as predicted by Moffitt's theory. The predictors were added to both predict latent class membership and the latent intercept and slope effects, see Figure 4 for an example of a model using gender as a predictor. Different prediction models were explored, including those with and without the latent class membership mediating the relationship of the predictors on the intercept and slopes.

As there are many specific research hypotheses suggested by Moffitt's developmental taxonomy. The following hypotheses were tested and are discussed in the following chapters by adding predictors on the growth factors:

1. LCPs should display evidence of behavioral problems in childhood across multiple domains.

2. LCPs should exhibit early physiological problems – e.g., diagnoses of ADD, ADHD, CD, other mental health diagnoses, etc.

3. LCPs should have experienced environmental and/or contextual difficulties and evidence of poor parenting and/or family dysfunction.

4. LCPs will have more suspensions and expulsions in childhood.

5. ALs should exhibit no differences on predictor variables in psychological or family factors from abstainers.

6. ALs should have more delinquent peer models.

7. ALs will be more heavily involved in drugs during adolescence.

8. ABs will evidence of resilience factors, such as self-esteem, strong family involvement, etc.

9. ABs will lack delinquent peer models and engage more with prosocial peers.

Figure 4. Example of a Model with Predictors

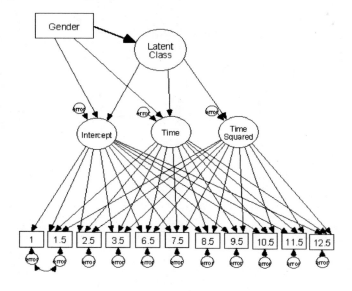

CHAPTER 4.

Baltimore Prevention Program

Data from the Second Generation of preventive intervention trials through the Johns Hopkins Center for Prevention and Early Intervention data was used to explore Moffitt's theory. The theoretical philosophies, design, and methodology of the preventive intervention trials are described in this chapter.

This research used data from the second generation of the Johns Hopkins University Prevention and Intervention Research Center's (PIRC) prevention intervention trials. Two classroom-based, universal preventive intervention programs were fielded in nine Baltimore City schools with a focus on the early risk behaviors of poor achievement and aggressive and shy behavior, and their distal correlates of antisocial behavior, substance abuse, and anxious and depressive symptoms. The data also include a comprehensive assessment of theoretically relevant family, school, peer, and individual characteristics at eleven measurement periods.

These field trials examined a set of school-based preventive interventions that were grounded in developmental epidemiology and Life Course/Social Field Theory. The first generation of trials began in 1985, the second generation built upon this work in 1993, and finally, the third generation of trials is currently underway in the Baltimore City School System.

The JHU PIRC second generation work, was supported by grants from the National Institute of Mental Health (Epidemiologic Prevention Center for Early Risk Behaviors, NIMH 5 PO MH38725, Sheppard G. Kellam, P.I.; Periodic Follow-up of Two Preventive Intervention Trials, RO 1 MH57005-02A, Nicholas S. Ialongo, P.I.) and the National Institute on Drug Abuse (NIDA RO1 DA11796-01A1, Nicholas S. Ialongo, P.I.). The principal collaborators have included Drs. Lisa Werthamer, Hendricks Brown, Sheppard G. Kellam, and Nicholas S. Ialongo. Nancy Karweit, Ph.D., Mary Alice Bond, M.A., Carolyn Webster-Stratton, Ph.D., Joyce Epstein, Ph.D., Irving Sigel, Ph.D., and Ruth Kandel, Ed.D. each made significant contributions to the development of the second generation JHU interventions. Their work is based on a theoretical framework integrating developmental epidemiology and Life Course/Social Field Theory, which are described below.

THEORETICAL FRAMEWORK

While epidemiology focuses on assessing the prevalence of disease and disorder and their correlates in specific populations, developmental epidemiology concentrates on following a sample or population over time to study variations in developmental courses. Developmental epidemiologists are interested in the differences in these developmental pathways and their correlates on multiple levels (such as individual and environmental factors), as well as the prospect of altering negative life-course trajectories through intervention.

Specifically for the work being done by the Baltimore Prevention Program, the developmental epidemiological framework allows the exploration of the variation in developmental trajectories in children with respect to academic success, socially adaptive or maladaptive behaviors, and mental health outcomes. This approach allows the investigation of antecedents, moderators, and outcomes in several areas that affect the overall well-being of the children being studied. With the identification of early mediating and moderating factors, interventions can be developed to alter the developmental trajectories.

The Baltimore Prevention Program applied the developmental epidemiological framework in conjunction with Life Course/Social Field Theory, a developmental framework than many researchers have found to be helpful when examining changes in individuals over their life spans (Kellam, Branch, Agrawal, & Ensminger, 1975; Kellam and Ensminger, 1980; Kellam and Rebok, 1992). Life Course/Social Field Theory posits that for each stage of life there are a few main social fields that constitute both present context and set the stage for future development. Typically, individuals are first involved primarily with their families, then in the school and their peer group. As they grow older, their dominant social fields shift to the workplace and its peer relations, the family of procreation with partner and children, and still later, their children's families become most salient. These key social fields are closely related to developmental life stages.

According to the Life Course/Social Field Theory, there are social task demands specific to each social field that establish an individual's competence, and there are people present in these social fields that can rate the individual's proficiency in each of these social task demands.

The social task demands of each key social field develop over the lifespan. For example, social task demands in early childhood include appropriate classroom behavior, such as sitting still, paying attention, and learning, while proper control of physical aggression and playing according to the rules of the game are important in social interactions with age mates. Peer relations soon take on a more salient role and social task demands such as getting along with others and establishing social bonds becomes more important in the success of an individual. Eventually, work and the family of procreation become more significant and different social task demands determine an individual's competence. Task demands in different social fields may overlap a great deal, but they are not inevitably identical and at times can be in conflict with one another.

Within each of these social fields with different social task demands, there are other people intimately involved with an individual and at a good position to observe his/her actions, successes, and failures. The ability to respond to different social task demands is reflected in an individual's social adaptational status, which is observed by the people involved in that life domain. These "natural raters," or people who can most accurately judge another's competence in a specific social field include parents in the family, teachers in the classroom, peers in the peer group, supervisors at work, and partners or spouses in the intimate/marital social field. In infancy through middle childhood, the primary caregivers are considered natural raters. Once a child enters school, a new social field, the classroom teacher becomes the natural rater of his/her success in the important task demands of school. Since an individual is generally involved in more than one major social field at a time, there are several available natural raters in different contexts at any point in an individual's life.

Each individual holds a unique set of strengths and weaknesses and these relate to his/her ability to adapt to social task demands. Successful social adaptation requires an individual to possess the capability to respond sufficiently to social task demands throughout his or her life span. Individuals who are performing their social task demands effectively possess high social adaptational status. According to the Life Course/Social Field Theory, early successful social adaptation tends to lead to success into later social fields because it builds on social, emotional, and cognitive competencies that can be used and transferred in new social fields. Mastery of social task demands reinforce positive social adaptation and the successful performance of task demands generalizes to later tasks that presuppose competence in other fields. Through this process, early competencies are used to master later task demands; and therefore, early positive social adaptation predicts later positive social adaptation. Conversely, early maladaptation can result in deficiencies and reinforces one's sense of failure and/or alienation.

INTERVENTIONS

The developmental epidemiological approach can explore the various influences that culture, broader social structure, community, and specific social fields such as classroom, family, neighborhood, and peer group have on the social task demands and the variation in social adaptational status. The prevention strategies tested in the Baltimore Prevention Program's preventive interventions were developed within this framework along with the Life Course/Social Field Theory, with a primary focus on the early social fields and individual variation in meeting the social task demands.

The developmental paths of children are influenced by the social field of the classroom and its social task demands by the teacher and classmates. The classroom interventions used in the Baltimore Preventive Intervention Trials target early maladaptive behavior that is hypothesized to influence later negative behaviors. Theoretically, improving social adaptation should decrease the risk of continuing maladaptive behavior through adolescence and adulthood. In the second generation of preventive intervention trials, the effectiveness of two interventions that were previously found to be effective in increasing social adaptational status.

Classroom Centered Intervention (CC)

The CC intervention consisted of three separate elements: (1) curricular enhancements; (2) improved classroom behavior management practices; and (3) supplementary strategies for children not performing adequately. The first component included enhancements to improve listening, comprehension, composition, critical thinking, and mathematic skills. Mastery learning is a teaching strategy based on Benjamin Bloom's model (Block, 1971). It is primarily a group-based, teacher-paced instructional approach which does not focus on content, but on the process of mastering it. While mastery learning incorporates a variety of group-based instructional techniques, it also incorporates frequent and specific feedback by both formal testing and the regular correction of mistakes. Teachers evaluate their students with criterion-referenced tests rather then norm-referenced tests which ensure numerous feedback loops, based on small units of well-defined, and appropriately sequenced outcomes.

The second component, classroom behavior management, incorporated a The Good Behavior Game (GBG) is a classroom management strategy designed to improve aggressive/disruptive classroom behavior and prevent later criminality. The program is a universal preventive intervention delivered to general populations of early elementary school children. Although it was designed for the general population, there is some evidence that the most noteworthy results were with children exhibiting early high-risk maladaptive behaviors. It was developed to be delivered in early elementary schools to provide students with the skills they need to respond to later life experiences and societal influences (e.g., increase early social adaptational status).

The Good Behavior Game is essentially a behavior modification program that involves students and teachers. It increases the teacher's capacity to define tasks, set rules, and discipline students. The game incorporates teamwork and mutual accountability to encourage students to reinforce positive behavior in one another. Students learn to conform to social expectations and increase their ability to complete their social task demands appropriately.

The final piece of the intervention included providing supplementary services to children who were identified as having additional needs. Specially trained tutors and counselors were made available when a child did not appear to be responding to the first two strategies.

Family-School Partnership (FSP)

The family-school partnership intervention (FSP) was designed to enhance parent-school communication and the parents; abilities to effectively manage their children's behavior. The major method for achieving those aims were (1) training for teachers/school mental health professionals and other relevant school staff in parent-school communication and partnership building (Canter & Canter, 1991), (2) weekly home-school learning and communication activities, and (3) a series of 9 workshops for parents led by the first grade teacher and the school psychologist or social worker.

The family-school partnership established effective and enduring partnership between parents and school staff to enable parents to get on board and provide a consistent message about academic and behavioral expectations. Workshops focused on improving the parents teaching and behavioral management skill so that they could support their children's academic achievement. Videotapes were also used to teach positive discipline (Webster-Stratton, 1984). Finally, a voice mail system that connected parents with their children's teachers helped to maintain parent involvement and positive reinforcement.

STUDY SAMPLE

In the fall of 1993, 678 urban first-graders were recruited from 27 classrooms in 9 elementary schools primarily located in western Baltimore. The first-graders ranged from 5.3 to 7.7 years of age in the beginning of the school year (M=6.2, SD=0.34). Parental consent was obtained for 97% of the children. Ninety-three percent of the children remained enrolled in project schools through grade 1 and completed the one-year intervention in their assigned intervention or control condition. The children were followed up for ten years, and 356, or 55.4%, were successfully followed for the entire span of the study period. Subjects with enough data were used for this study and the intervention effects will be considered in all analyses.

The 678 students were assigned to one of three conditions: (1) control classrooms (N=220), (2) classroom centered intervention classrooms (N=230), and (3) family-school partnership intervention classrooms (N=228). Schools were used as the randomized blocking factor and students and teachers were randomly assigned to conditions. The intervention was delivered for the duration of the first grade year. The students were dispersed to different classrooms and schools for the remainder of the study period. The interventions were found to be successful at reducing substance use, mental health problems, and aggressive and shy/withdrawn behaviors. For a review of the major findings from this study, see Furr-Holden et al., 2004, Ialongo et al., 1999, Lambert, Ialongo, Boyd and Cooley, 2005, and Storr, Ialongo, Kellam, and Anthony, 2002.

The second generation of the Prevention and Intervention Research Center's intervention and follow-up began when youth entered the first grade in 1993. Over the span of these ten years, subject attrition occurred and must be considered. In early years, there were no differences between those youth followed between first and second grade in terms of intervention condition, socio-demographic characteristics, or baseline levels of academic achievement and parent or teacher ratings of child behaviors. According to previous analyses, boys with missing data at the second wave of follow-up did differ than those with complete records in their teacher ratings of problem behaviors in the fall or spring of first grade. In terms of more distal outcomes, as has been previously noted, there were no differences in those surveyed and those lost to follow-up at waves six through eight with respect to teacher ratings, academic achievement, race/ethnicity, sex, or free lunch status (Furr-Holden et al., 2004).

Figure 5. *Sample Size*

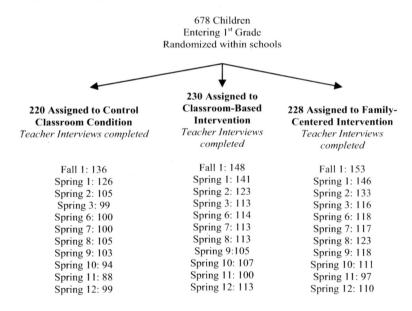

678 Children
Entering 1st Grade
Randomized within schools

220 Assigned to Control Classroom Condition	**230 Assigned to Classroom-Based Intervention**	**228 Assigned to Family-Centered Intervention**
Teacher Interviews completed	*Teacher Interviews completed*	*Teacher Interviews completed*
Fall 1: 136	Fall 1: 148	Fall 1: 153
Spring 1: 126	Spring 1: 141	Spring 1: 146
Spring 2: 105	Spring 2: 123	Spring 2: 133
Spring 3: 99	Spring 3: 113	Spring 3: 116
Spring 6: 100	Spring 6: 114	Spring 6: 118
Spring 7: 100	Spring 7: 113	Spring 7: 117
Spring 8: 105	Spring 8: 113	Spring 8: 123
Spring 9: 103	Spring 9: 105	Spring 9: 118
Spring 10: 94	Spring 10: 107	Spring 10: 111
Spring 11: 88	Spring 11: 100	Spring 11: 97
Spring 12: 99	Spring 12: 113	Spring 12: 110

ASSESSMENT STRATEGY

In order to test Moffitt's taxonomy of offending, appropriate measurements of offending (antisocial behavior, delinquency, or other such manifestation of criminality) and Moffitt's theoretically-relevant predictors had to be selected. This dataset provided a wealth of information, which included both official and self-report measures of antisocial and maladaptive behavior. The official reports included school records (including standardized achievement scores, grades, and disciplinary actions, among others), and unofficial reports include student self-reports, and teacher and family ratings of behavior.

The sample demographic table below provides details about each of the data collection periods with respect to intervention status, sex, race, socioeconomic status, and family structure. The subjects were evenly split between the intervention conditions in the fall of first grade and while the percentage of missing data differs across measurement period, the proportion of each of the three intervention statuses at different time periods did not appear to differ significantly overall, see table below (Control: mean=31.67%, 95% CI =31.32%-32.15%; CC: mean=33.43, 95% CI=32.54%-34.31%; FSP: mean=33.71, 95% CI=33.30%-34.12%). The gender composition of the sample is almost evenly split, with a slight majority being male at the first data collection period (male = 53.4%, female = 46.6%). This difference persists throughout the study period (males: mean=53.35%. 95% CI=52.00%-54.71%; females=46.65%, 95% CI=45.29%-48.00%). The sample was predominantly made up of Black/African-American students (86.3% at entrance into first grade) at all data collection points.

The average age of the subjects upon entering first grade is six years old (M=6.23, SD=0.37) with the minimum age being almost five years old and the maximum age of eight. Approximately one-quarter of the sample come from families with annual incomes of less than $10,000, another quarter from families with annual incomes between $10,000 and $20,000, the third quarter from families with annual incomes between $20,000 and $30,000, and the final quarter from families who earn over $30,000 per year. Approximately half of the children live with two parents or caregivers (including step parents and other adults living in the residence).

Table 1. Sample Demographic Profile

	Fall 1st	Sp 1st	2nd	3rd	6th	7th	8th	9th	10th	11th	12th
N: Overall	678	648	560	509	569	577	583	551	522	398	443
Control	32.3	31.6	30.5	32.0	31.5	31.0	31.9	32.7	31.8	32.2	31.6
Classroom	33.9	34.3	34.3	34.6	32.5	32.6	31.6	32.1	31.8	35.2	34.8
Family	33.8	34.1	35.2	33.4	33.7	33.6	33.8	33.2	33.7	32.7	33.6
Sex: Male	53.4	53.2	52.7	51.3	54.8	55.6	54.7	55.7	54.8	50.0	50.6
Female	46.6	46.8	47.3	48.7	45.2	44.4	45.3	44.3	45.2	50.0	49.4
Race: Black	86.3	86.4	88.9	89.6	86.6	86.1	86.4	87.1	87.0	88.9	88.5
White	13.6	13.6	11.1	10.4	13.4	13.9	13.6	12.9	13.0	11.1	11.5
Income: <$5K	11.5	10.8									
$5K-$10K	15.5	9.5									
$10K-20K	20.9	21.7									
$20K-30K	18.5	21.4									
$30K-50K	20.3	21.1									
Family: 2 Parents[3]	49.3	46.0			39.6	40.7	44.7	44.0			
1 Parent[4]	43.5	46.2			51.8	49.9	45.0	46.7			

[3] Two parents includes: (1) mother and father only, (2) mother and step-father, (3) father and step-mother, (4) or mother and father with other adults living in the residents.

[4] One parent includes the combination of the following household members: (1) mother alone, (2) father alone, (3) mother and any other adult(s), (4) father and any other adults(s)

CHAPTER 5.

Measuring Delinquency

Since Moffitt's taxonomy focuses on delinquent behavior, a composite score of delinquency was developed from multiple items. According to Moffitt (1993; 1994), a broad range of criminal and antisocial behaviors must be considered to test her theory. Many researchers have used childhood antisocial behavior (e.g., conduct disorder) to extend the left-hand side of the censored age-crime curve (Loeber, Stouthamer-Loeber, Van Kammen, & Farrington, 1989). With the inclusion of these alternative measurements of antisocial behavior and self-report measures, researchers have uncovered higher rates of illegal and antisocial behavior (Elliott, Ageton, Huizinga, Knowles, & Canter, 1983). In fact, Nagin, Farrington, and Moffitt (1995) found very different patterns in offenders using official verses self-report data. The self-report data was much richer and demonstrated that many offenders who appeared to be desisting from crime were actually just not being captured by official data. Therefore, this study will use not rely solely on official data.

The dataset offers several options for defining delinquency at different ages. This study will use teacher ratings of delinquency using the Aggressive/Disruptive Subscale from the TOCA-R because this measurement was recorded at most of the data collection time periods, and it has also been found to be a highly valid and reliable measure of aggression. It also represents the social adaptational status and competency of the child at meeting the social task demands in the classroom, which is a research-validated antecedent of delinquencyThe main dependent variable in the study, delinquency, was defined using teacher (the natural rater of the classroom social field) reports of aggressive behavior.

The Teacher Observation of Classroom Adaptation – Revised (TOCA-R; Werthamer-Larsson et al., 1991) was designed to assess each child's adequacy of performance on the core task demands in the classroom. It involves a structured interview administered by a trained evaluator. The interviewer records the teacher's rating of the adequacy of each student's performance on three core tasks: authority acceptance (the maladaptive form being aggressive/delinquent behavior); social participation (shy behavior); and concentration and being ready for work (the maladaptive form being concentration problems). Teachers rate the students on a six-point frequency scale (1: not at all, 6: always). The scale used in this study, the aggression/disruption scale, includes items on breaking classroom rules, damaging property, starting fights, among others. The coefficient alpha on the TOCA-R aggressive/ disruptive scale was .94. The one year test-retest reliability ranged from .65 to .79 over grades 2-3, 3-4, and 4-5. In terms of concurrent validity, the aggressive/disruptive scale was significantly related to the incidence of school suspensions within each year in elementary school in the 1st generation of JHU PIRC trails (Kellam et al., 1994).

As previously discussed, delinquency is measured by teacher observations using the Teacher Observation of Classroom Adaptation – Revised (TOCA-R; Werthamer-Larsson et al., 1991), which measures aggressive behavior exhibited in the classroom. The aggression/ disruption subscale is made up of slightly different items for different time periods, reflecting a difference in the manifestation of aggressive/disruptive behavior across time that reflects the change in the developmental construct from childhood through adolescence. In the early years (first through third grade) the scale is made up the average of eleven items, rated on a six-point frequency scale, and in adolescence, the scale is made up of the average of only five of the eleven items using in the previous years.

The average of the teachers ratings of each subject (1=Never, 2=Almost Never, 3=Rarely, 4=Often, 5=Very Often, 6=Always) of each item was computed to make the Aggression/ Disruption Subscale. According to previous research using the same scale, the coefficient alpha on the TOCA-R aggressive/disruptive scale was .94. The one year test-retest reliability ranged from .65 to .79 over grades 2-3, 3-4, and 4-5. In terms of concurrent validity, the aggressive/disruptive scale was significantly related to the incidence of school suspensions within each year in elementary school in the 1st generation of JHU PIRC trials (Kellam et al., 1994).

At the first data collection period, the average delinquency score was 1.62, which translates to an "almost never" response category – meaning that on average, the students almost never displayed aggressive/disruptive behavior in the fall of the first grade. The delinquency ratings peaked in third grade with a mean of 1.90 and were the lowest in the final data collection period, twelfth grade with a mean of 1.44, see figure below. The range of delinquency scores narrowed as the sample aged; by middle school no one was rated above 5.10 and by high school the maximum delinquency score did not rise above a 4.80.

Table 2. *Aggression/Disruption Scale, TOCA-R*

First through Third Grade (1991-1993)	Sixth through Twelfth Grades (1999 – 2005)
1) Stubborn	1) Broke Rules
2) Breaks Rules	2) Hurt Others Physically
3) Harms or Hurts Others Physically	3) Damaged Other People's Property on Purpose
4) Harms or Damages Property on Purpose	4) Took Others Property
5) Breaks Things	5) Lied
6) Yells at Others	
7) Takes Others Property	
8) Fights	
9) Lies	
10) Talk Back to Adults/Disrespectful	
11) Teases Classmates	

Figure 6. Mean Delinquency Rating and 95% Confidence Intervals by Grade

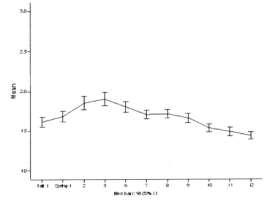

The delinquency scores were not normally distributed at any of the measurement periods. The scores were significantly positively skewed (meaning it has a longer tail on the positive side) and leptokurtotic (meaning that it has a sharper peak than the normal distribution), both of which violate the assumptions for most parametric statistics; however, this is not a problem for group-based trajectory modeling as it assumes that there are multiple normal distributions represented. Since there are multiple latent distributions, the skewness is assumed to be an artifact of the underlying distributions. Therefore, no transformations were performed on the variables to normalize the delinquency scores; but it should be recognized that any parametric statistics performed on these variables may be biased by the considerable skewness, kurtosis, and abundance of outliers.

Table 3. Mean Delinquency Scores and Percent of Missing Data

Measurement Period	Mean (SD)	Min-Max	Skewness (SE)	Kurtosis (SE)	% Missing
Fall First	1.62 (.85)	1 – 6.00	2.04 (.09)	4.35 (.19)	15.1%
Spring First	1.68 (.87)	1 - 6.00	1.84 (.10)	3.63 (.19)	18.9%
Spring Second	1.85 (.99)	1 - 5.91	1.45 (.10)	1.84 (.21)	29.9%
Spring Third	1.90 (.94)	1 - 5.27	1.20 (.11)	.90 (.22)	36.0%
Spring Sixth	1.84 (.81)	1 - 5.10	1.54 (.10)	2.43 (.20)	28.8%
Spring Seventh	1.73 (.70)	1 - 4.73	1.37 (.10)	1.78 (.20)	27.8%
Spring Eighth	1.74 (.69)	1 - 4.40	1.26 (.10)	1.24 (.20)	27.0%
Spring Ninth	1.67 (.72)	1 - 4.80	1.75 (.10)	3.37 (.21)	31.0%
Spring Tenth	1.57 (.59)	1 - 4.80	1.89 (.11)	7.74 (.21)	34.7%
Spring Eleventh	1.48 (.53)	1 - 4.20	1.74 (.12)	3.49 (.24)	50.0%
Spring Twelfth	1.44 (.49)	1 - 4.40	2.05 (.12)	6.18 (.23)	44.6%

It is unclear whether this decline in delinquency scores and range restriction are related to the missing data; perhaps those with the highest delinquency scores were most likely to drop out of the study. Over the span of these twelve years, subject attrition occurred and must be considered. The teacher ratings of delinquency are missing for a minimum of 15% of the subjects (fall of first grade) to a maximum of 50% (spring of grade 11), with an average of 31% of the data missing at any one measurement point.

The manner in which missing data will be dealt with is extremely important for these analyses. It does not appear that missingness is related to early aggression scores, see table below for Kendall's Tau correlations between aggression scores in the fall and spring of first grade and missing data in six through twelfth grades. The only significant relationships are in the final two years of the study period, and the tau's are extremely low; however, they do provide limited evidence that individuals with higher early scores on the aggression/disruption scale may be more likely to have missing data in the last two years of high school. Of course, this does not rule-out the possibility of there being other correlates and patterns of missing data, related to either aggression/disruption or another source, such as school drop-out. The ramifications of missing data on the analyses will be discussed more fully in the final chapter.

Table 4. *Kendall's Tau Relationship Between Delinquency in Early Years and Missing Data*

	Delinquency Score Fall First Grade	Delinquency Score Spring First Grade
Missing Sixth Grade	-.03	-.03
Missing Seventh Grade	-.04	-.03
Missing Eighth Grade	-.04	-.05
Missing Ninth Grade	-.05	-.03
Missing Tenth Grade	-.03	-.05
Missing Eleventh Grade	-.06	-.07*
Missing Twelfth Grade	-.08*	-.10*

* significant at p<.05

DELINQUENCY BY INTERVENTION STATUS

The mean delinquency scores by intervention status were equal across the groups at each time period except the fall of first grade (before the intervention was delivered) and the eleventh grade. The children in the Classroom Centered Intervention had the highest baseline aggression/disruption scores, and the children in the Control Group had the highest scores in the eleventh grade follow-up, even after adjusting for inflated alpha levels. These differences disappeared in the subsequent measurement period, and it is unclear why there were group differences at these specific time points and not others.

Table 5. Delinquency Scores by Intervention Status

	Fall 1st	Sp 1st	2nd	3rd	6th	7th	8th	8th	10th	11h	12th
Control											
Mean	1.49	1.63	1.89	1.91	1.89	1.76	1.75	1.66	1.62	1.63	1.50
(SD)	(.80)	(.82)	(.95)	(.98)	(.84)	(.69)	(.69)	(.65)	(.63)	(.66)	(.56)
Max	5.82	4.82	5.91	5.27	5.10	4.20	4.40	4.40	4.20	4.20	4.40
N	219	205	171	163	179	179	186	180	166	128	140
CC											
Mean	1.78	1.63	1.80	1.90	1.80	1.71	1.71	1.71	1.57	1.43	1.44
(SD)	(.98)	(.93)	(1.0)	(.92)	(.81)	(.76)	(.65)	(.81)	(.57)	(.47)	(.49)
Max	6	5.18	5.36	5	5	4.20	4.10	4.80	4.50	3.33	4.00
N	230	222	192	176	185	188	184	177	166	140	154
FSP											
Mean	1.57	1.78	1.87	1.89	1.79	1.71	1.73	1.65	1.49	1.39	1.38
(SD)	(.73)	(.86)	(1.0)	(.92)	(.75)	(.67)	(.68)	(.67)	(.56)	(.42)	(.41)
Max	4.64	6.00	5.91	5.00	5.10	4.33	4.20	4.20	4.8	2.80	3.10
N	229	221	197	170	192	194	197	183	176	130	149
ANOVA	6.74	2.02	.489	.035	1.52	1.04	2.17	.60	2.45	7.80	2.24
P value	001*	0.13	0.48	0.97	0.21	0.37	0.09	0.61	0.06	0.01*	0.11

DELINQUENCY BY GENDER

There was a significant difference in mean delinquency ratings between males and females at each data collection period. Males always displayed higher mean levels of aggression/disruption, which is consistent with prior research (Mears, Ploeger, & Warr, 1988). Females scored approximately 0.4 points below males at each data collection period, and they were more homogeneous in their ratings than their male counterparts. It is also interesting to note that despite their obvious differences, they followed the same general pattern across time – increasing through third grade, and then decreasing from middle through high school, see figure below.

Figure 7. **Mean Delinquency Ratings by Gender**

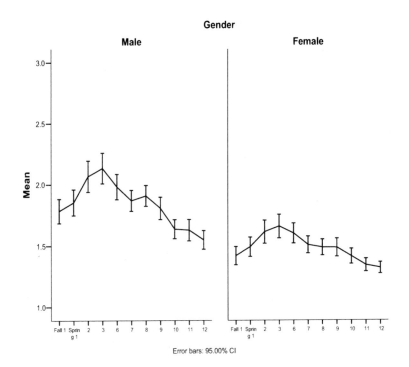

Error bars: 95.00% CI

Table 6. Delinquency Ratings by Gender

	Fall 1st	Sp 1st	2nd	3rd	6th	7th	8th	8th	10th	11h	12th
Male Mean	1.78	1.81	1.89	2.13	2.02	1.90	1.94	1.81	1.68	1.63	1.55
(SD)	(.96)	(1.0)	(1.0)	(1.0)	(.90)	(.77)	(.75)	(.78)	(.65)	(.62)	(.57)
Max	6	5.18	5.91	5.27	5.10	4.73	4.40	4.80	4.80	4.20	4.40
N	362	88	62	261	312	321	319	307	286	199	224
Female Mean (SD)	1.42	1.66	1.85	1.66	1.61	1.52	1.50	1.50	1.43	1.34	1.32
	(.67)	(.84)	(.99)	(.76)	(.62)	(.54)	(.50)	(.58)	(.47)	(.38)	(.35)
Max	5.55	6	5.91	4.27	5	4	4	4.20	4.20	3.20	2.86
N	316	560	498	248	257	256	264	244	236	199	219
ANOVA	32.0	2.25	0.11	34.6	37.2	43.6	68.0	27.2	23.6	29.5	25.3
p-value	0.01	0.14	0.75	0.01	0.01	0.01	0.01	0.01	0.01	0.01	0.01

DELINQUENCY BY RACE

The mean delinquency scores did not differ by race. The overwhelming majority of subjects in this study were Black/African-American and there was very little racial variation. There was only one Hispanic individual, who was dropped from this analysis. There were no Asian, Pacific Islanders, or any other minority group, and therefore, it is impossible to draw any inferences about any other groups. This analysis suggests that White/Caucasians and Black/African-Americans display equal amounts of aggressive/disruptive behavior in the classroom. The larger amount of variation in the White groups is likely due to the relatively small sample size.

Table 7. Delinquency Ratings by Race

	Fall 1st	Sp 1st	2nd	3rd	6th	7th	8th	8th	10th	11h	12th
White											
Mean (SD)	1.64	1.81	1.89	1.83	1.76	1.72	1.64	1.53	1.54	1.40	1.35
	(.97)	(1.06)	(1.06)	(.95)	(.84)	(.74)	(.64)	(.61)	(.56)	(.44)	(.34)
Max	5	5.18	5.91	4.55	5	3.50	3.30	3.60	3.60	2.85	2.50
N	92	88	62	53	76	80	79	71	68	44	51
Black Mean (SD)	1.61	1.66	1.85	1.91	1.85	1.73	1.76	1.70	1.59	1.50	1.45
	(.84)	(.84)	(.99)	(.94)	(.80)	(.70)	(.69)	(.73)	(.59)	(.54)	(.51)
Max	6	6	5.91	5.27	5.10	4.73	4.40	4.8	4.80	4.20	4.40
N	585	560	498	456	493	497	504	480	454	354	392
ANOVA	0.20	2.25	0.11	0.37	0.71	0.02	1.97	3.29	0.13	1.15	1.76
p-value	0.82	0.14	0.75	0.54	0.40	0.90	0.16	0.07	0.72	0.29	0.19

COVARIATES

Covariates will be used to predict group membership and the intercept and slope effects. The covariates were selected on the basis of their relevance in testing Moffitt's developmental taxonomy. The Johns Hopkins University Prevention Intervention Research Center's data includes several variables that represent applicable constructs that are hypothesized to be related to life-course-persistent offending and adolescence-limited offending.

Due to the way in which Mplus estimates the effects of covariates in General Growth Mixture Models, any case with missing data on a covariate will be dropped from the analysis, which makes picking covariates more complex (Muthén & Muthén, 1998-2004). Therefore, all efforts will be made to get complete data on each covariate.

The variables selected to serve as predictors of the group-based group curves are those that most closely aligned with Moffitt's theory. There are individual-level, peer-level, and family-level predictors that will be explored. Every effort will be made to use variables that are directly hypothesized to be causal factors of the different growth trajectories.

Individual Predictors
1. The *TOCA-R* provides information from classroom teachers about attention/concentration problems, hyperactivity, and impulsivity, each of which are indicative of psycho-physiological problems.
2. Psychological problems, such as anxiety and depression, are measured by the *Baltimore How I Feel—Young Child Version* (Ialongo, Kellam, & Poduska, 1999).

Peer Predictors
1. *Exposure to Deviant Peers* (Capaldi & Patterson, 1989) measures the deviant behavior of each individual's peer group (coefficient alphas ranged from .78 to .81 in 1985-86 JHU PIRC cohorts in middle school).
2. The *Neighborhood Environment Scale* will be used to measure exposure to deviant behavior in the neighborhood (Elliott, Huizinga, & Ageton, 1985).

3. *Harter Close Friendship Scale* provides a measure of how much importance in placed in close friendships, which is a proxy measure for social bonding (Harter, 1985)

Family Predictors

1. Household structure and demographics, collected in first and sixth through tenth grades, will be used to measure marital status, ethnicity, employment status, as well as family income, and biological father's and mother's involvement in caregiving.
2. *Parent Discipline* and *Parent Monitoring* are measured through parent interviews to determine level of parental involvement and environmental dysfunction in childhood.

Life-Course-Persistent Offender Covariates

Moffitt hypothesized that there would be a confluence of both individual and environmental dysfunction for an individual to become a life-course-persistent offender. Therefore, at least one of each type of predictors should be present in the life-course-persistent offender – individual and/or environmental pathology. Moffitt provided examples of the types of problems that could lead to life-course-persistent offending; however, her theory did not take a deterministic stance. Therefore, her hypothesized etiology was not rigid, but rather allowed for many different combinations and patterns of pathologies. The most important part of her theory is that there is the presence of irregularity in both realms.

According to Moffitt, life-course-persistent offenders display evidence of early physiological problems, such as attention deficit disorder (ADD), attention deficit/hyperactivity disorder (ADHD), conduct disorder (CD), or other mental health or cognition problems. For this analysis, teacher ratings of hyperactivity and concentration as well as child reports of anxious and depressive symptoms will be used to measure psychological problems (see Appendix A for questions and the item coding of the scales).

A *Teacher Ratings of Concentration Scale* was computed using the TOCA-R over the first four data collection periods in order to minimize missing data. The scale is reliable (Chronbach's alpha = .84) and therefore, if a subject had a score on at least two data collection periods, the average across the available time periods was used. Over sixty percent of the sample had teacher ratings at all data collection periods, 11% were rated at three of the four time periods, 10% had ratings at two points, and 18% only had one or fewer ratings and were therefore counted as missing.

A *Teacher Ratings of Hyperactivity Scale* was computed from the TOCA-R over the first four data collection periods. The scale is reliable (Chronbach's alpha = .87), and therefore, if a subject had a score for at least two data collection periods, the average across the available time periods was used. As this rating was collected at the same time as the Teacher Ratings of Concentration Scale, the missing data information is the same as previously reported.

A *Self-Report Anxiety Scale* was computed from the Baltimore How I Feel Scale over the first four data collection periods. The scale reliability is lower than for the previous two scales, which could be due to the fact that either anxiety is less stable over time or the measurement is not reliable (Chronbach's alpha =.53). A score was computed for each subject that had at least two anxiety scores during the four collection periods. Fifty-six percent of the sample had anxiety scores for all four data collection periods, 12% had three, 9.5% had two, and the remaining 22% had one or no anxiety scores on the Baltimore How I Feel Scale during the first four data collection periods.

A *Self-Report Depression Scale* was computed from the Baltimore How I Feel Scale over the first four data collection periods. The scale reliability is lower, which could be due to the fact that depression is less stable over time or the measurement is less reliable (Chronbach's alpha =.56). A score was computed for each subject that had at least two depression scores during the four collection periods. As this scale was collected at the same time as the Self-Report Anxiety Scale, the missing data information is the same for both scales.

Environmental/parental dysfunction was measured through parental practices. Two scales were collected from parent interviews – the *Parent Discipline* and *Parent Monitoring* scales. Both of these scales were collected at two points in time, the fall and spring of the first grade. The average of the scales over the two years was taken for both of them to increase the reliability and decrease the percentage of missing data. The Parental Discipline scale was fairly reliable (Chronbach's alpha = .70), but the Parental Monitoring scale had a very low reliability over the two measurement periods (Chronbach's alpha

=.35). The parent discipline measured how consistent a parent is in disciplining their child when he or she does something wrong. A higher score represents a child that is less consistently disciplined, and the average score of 2.03 represents a score of "hardly ever" letting a child get away with doing something wrong. Parental monitoring was measured by four items about awareness of their children's actions outside of their supervision. The low reliability could be that the first measurement was taken in the fall of the first grade, when there was very little time during which the parents could have been made aware of their children's behavior in school. The descriptive statistics for all of the scales are provided in the table below.

Table 8. *Predictors of Life-Course-Persistent Offenders*

Covariate	Mean (SD)	Min-Max	Skew (SE)	Kurtosis (SE)	% Miss
Concentration	2.84 (1.17)	1-5.83	.29 (.10)	-.80 (.19)	8.6%
Hyperactivity	2.12 (.95)	1-5.83	1.14 .10)	.84 (.19)	8.6%
Anxiety	.78 (.25)	.05-1.65	.03 (.10)	-.04 (.20)	4.3%
Depression	.76 (.23)	.18-1.42	.05 (.10)	-.34 (.20)	4.3%
Discipline	2.03 (.68)	1 – 5	.68 (.10)	.42 (.20)	8.5%
Monitoring	1.15 (.30)	1 – 4	3.66 (.10)	19.89 (.20)	8.6%

The relationships between all the life-course-persistent offender predictor variables were explored to make sure that there would be no problems with multicollinearity. Two of the hypothesized predictors of life-course-persistent offending were moderately correlated with the observed measurements of delinquency at each time period, the concentration and hyperactivity scales. The anxiety, depression, and parental discipline scales were not related to individual measurements of delinquency. The parental monitoring scale was related at the three of the measurement periods, but these relationships were very small (r=0.09-0.11). However, there are a couple of issues that could prevent relationships from appearing even though they exist: (1) the scales could be related to delinquency trajectories, which are not discernable at any single measurement periods, and (2) some of the scales have very low reliability (depression, anxiety, and parental monitoring).

There is a compelling reason to believe that the relationships between concentration, hyperactivity and delinquency will be inflated – the correlation could be reflecting a correlated error terms since they are measured by the same raters (classroom teachers). However, since the measures of concentration and hyperactivity are averaged over four time periods, three of which are taken by different classroom teachers, the problem with correlated error terms should be reduced.

Table. 9. Correlation between Adolescence-Limiting Offending Predictors and Delinquency Scores

Scale	F1	Sp1	2	3	6	7	8	9	10	11	12
Concen	.45	.44	.47	.46	.42	.32	.39	.40	.32	.29	.30
Hyper	.60	.60	.62	.57	.44	.35	.43	.37	.29	.24	.24
Anxiety	-.03	-.06	.00	-.03	-.02	.01	-.06	.06	-.03	.06	-.01
Depress	.04	-.02	.04	.05	.02	.04	-.02	.09	.04	-02	-.02
Disc	-.04	-.02	-.02	.03	.07	.01	.04	.01	-.03	-.07	-.01
Monitor	.04	.02	.06	.06	.09	.11	.02	-.01	.06	.11	.02

Adolescence-Limited Offender Covariates

A measure of *Exposure to Deviant Peers* was used to determine if the individuals in the sample had access to deviant peer role models, as predicted by Moffitt's Taxonomy. Patterson and colleagues (1992) have theorized that drift into a deviant peer group increases the risk for antisocial behavior. They argue that antisocial behavior is not only modeled but also reinforced by the deviant peers. Accordingly, using a scale developed by Capaldi and Patterson, youths were asked in forced choice format to indicate how often their peers have engaged in antisocial behavior. Coefficient alphas ranged from .78 to .81 in the 1985-86 JHU PIRC cohorts during the middle school years. This measure was taken in 6th through 12th grades, and a scale was computed as the average score over the time period. The average of all the available time periods was used, as long as it was collected for at least three of the seven time periods because of the high reliability of the scale (Chronbach's alpha = 0.79), which reduced the missing data to only 16%.

A measure of *Neighborhood* was taken through Youth Interviews to quantify the criminogenic context in which the youths resided during adolescence. A structured interview measured neighborhood environment through ten questions about the youth's perceptions of drug use, safety, and property crime in his or her neighborhood. The perceptions were then averaged from sixth through tenth grade to create a very reliable scale (Chronbach's alpha=0.88). The average score was 1.73 which represents a neighborhood with negative statements about crime being "a little true" and a high score being more deviant. The descriptive statistics for each of the adolescence-limited predictors are provided below.

Table 10. Predictors of Adolescence-Limited Offenders

Covariate	Mean (SD)	Min-Max	Skew (SE)	Kurtosis (SE)	% Missing
Deviant Peers	1.55 (.42)	1 – 3.53	1.37 (.10)	2.59 (.20)	15.9%
Neighborhood	1.73 (.49)	1 – 3.61	.69 (.10)	-.05 (.20)	15.9%

Both of the hypothesized predictors of adolescence-limited offending appear to be related to the individual measurements of delinquency. According to the theory, these covariates should be related to delinquency in adolescence, but not in childhood. Looking at the bivariate relationships, it does appear that they are more strongly correlated with delinquency in middle and high schools, see table below. The correlations range from small (r=.11) to moderate (r=.46).

Table 11. Correlation between Adolescence-Limited Offending Predictors and Delinquency Scores

Scale	1Fall	1Spring	2	3	6	7
Deviant Peers	.11*	.08	.09	.06	.11*	.14**
Neighborhood	-.02	.21**	.17**	.21**	.27**	.31**

	8	9	10	11	12
Deviant Peers	.18**	.15**	.16**	.11*	.24**
Neighborhood	.27**	.38**	.32**	.46**	.63

* significant at the p<.05 level

** significant at the p<0.001

Abstainer Covariates

Moffitt's theory is much less developed with respect to the abstainers. She predicted that these individuals would not experience the maturity gap to the same extent as their adolescence-limited counterparts. This could either be from a postponement of physical maturity, lack of delinquent role models, or some other experience of social maturity and/or recognition that closes the maturity gap. To truly test this theory, indicators of physical maturity that are not available are necessary. The only proxy for any of Moffitt's predictors is the ***Harter Close Friendship Importance Subscale***, which measures how much importance a respondent places on friendship. This is a measurement of social bonding, which has been found to be a protective factor against delinquency. This scale was composed of the Harter Close Friendship Importance Scale averaged over grades 6 through 12 (Chronbach's Alpha=.80). The average score was just above 3, with higher scores reflecting a stronger importance placed on social bonds with peers.

Table 12. *Predictors of Abstaining*

Covariate	Mean (SD)	Min-Max	Skew (SE)	Kurtosis (SE)	% Miss
Close Friends	3.16 (.70)	1.14 – 5.57	-.58 (.10)	-.30 (.20)	15.9%

The Harter Close Friendship Importance Scale, averaged over six years, was related to individual delinquency scores in middle and high school, although the relationships were small (ranging from -0.11 to -0.19). It appears that the more importance a subject places in friendships, the less delinquent behavior he/she displays in the classroom.

Table 13. *Correlation between Abstaining Predictors and Delinquency*

Scale	1Fall	1Spring	2	3	6	7
Close Friends	-.01	-.03	-.10*	-.08	-.12*	-.11*

	8	9	10	11	12
Close Friends	-.19*	-.13*	-.15*	-.13*	-.11*

* significant at the p<.05 level
** significant at the p<0.001

Covariate Relationships

The covariates, for the most part, were not highly correlated with one another. As would be expected, hyperactivity and concentration were moderately-to-highly correlated (r=.55), but again, these scores were taken by the same raters, and therefore the correlation coefficient is likely to be inflated due to correlated errors terms. Anxiety and depression are also highly correlated, share 56% of their variation, but are not related to concentration or hyperactivity. Again, these psychological construct measurements are taken by the same rater (the child), and therefore display an inflated relationship due to correlated error terms. Interestingly, parental monitoring and discipline practices do not appear to be related to any of the other covariates, or even each other, but the ability to uncover a relationship is greatly handicapped by the poor scale reliability.

Table 14. Correlation between Offender Covariates

	Conc	Hype	Anx	Dep	Monit	Disc	Peers	Neigh
Hyper	.55**							
Anx	.11**	-.03						
Dep	-.03	.05	.75**					
Monitor	-.02	.06	-.03	-.03				
Disc	.06	-.02	.06	.06	.01			
Peers	.02	.06	.04	.04	.07	.03		
Neighbor	.09**	.17**	.07	.07	.02	.06	.31**	
Friend	-.01	-.05	-.06	-.06	-.002	-.03	-.04	-.20**

* significant at the $p<.05$ level

** significant at the $p<0.001$

The adolescence-limited predictors, deviant peer affiliation and neighborhood context, are moderately correlated ($r=0.31$). This is not surprising since more deviant peers would be available in a more troubled neighborhood. Neighborhood also has a small but significant relationship to concentration and hyperactivity, but deviant peer affiliation does not appear to be related to either of these constructs. Neighborhood also shares a small relationship with the importance that an individual places on friendship ($r=-0.20$) which means those who perceive a more criminogenic neighborhood are less likely to place great importance on friendship and place less importance on their peers.

After examining the covariates and their relationships with both delinquency and each other, there do not appear to be any problems entering them into a growth model as predictors of latent class. While several of the predictors do not share bivariate relationships with the measurements of delinquency, they could still be associated with the growth factors. There should be no problems with multicollinearity. Each covariate will be entered into the model regardless of its bivariate relationship with the dependent measures.

CHAPTER 6.

Developmental Trajectories

One of the primary questions that was explored in this research was whether group-based trajectory modeling captures the development of antisocial behavior over time better than a single group general growth model. Simply stated, the first question was whether everyone experiences a similar developmental course or if there are groups that display comparable growth trajectories that are distinct from one another. This was explored using Mplus Version 4.2.

First, a general growth model was run ignoring intervention condition to determine the shape of the developmental trajectories overall and establish the number of latent parameters needed to capture the growth process. Even though the analysis of each of the dependent variables suggested that the three groups could be combined in the growth curve mode, the differences between the conditions on the latent growth parameters was explored to determine whether intervention status alters the shape of the growth process and whether separate models will have to be run on each intervention group. The following indicators were used to determine which model was the best fit:

1. ***Tucker-Lewis Coefficient*** (TLI: Bentler, 1988) is also called the Bentler-Bonett non-normed fit index (NNFI). TLI is not guaranteed to vary from 0 to 1. TLI close to 1 indicates a good fit and those that have .90 or higher are considered acceptable, and above .95 is very good. The TLI is calculated:

$$\frac{\chi^2 / df \text{ (Null Model)} - \chi^2 / df \text{ (Alternative Model)}}{\chi^2 / df \text{ (Null Model)}}$$

2. ***Comparative Fit Index*** (CFI: Bentler, 1988) assesses model fit using a noncentral χ^2 distribution. The CFI is normed to a 0 – 1 range and values greater than .95 are indicative of good-fitting models. Models about .90 are considered acceptable. The CFI is calculated:

$$\frac{|\chi^2 - df\ (\text{Null Model})| - |\chi^2 - df\ (\text{Alt Model})|}{\chi^2 - df\ (\text{Null Model})}$$

3. ***Root Mean Square Error of Approximation*** (RMSEA: Browne & Cudeck, 1993) estimates the lack of model fit between a hypothesized model and the saturated model. Values larger than .10 indicate poor-filling models. The RMSEA is calculated: $\sqrt{[\ \chi^2 /\ (df\text{-}1)/(n-1)]}$

4. ***Akaike Information Criterion*** (AIC: Akaike, 1987) assesses model fit and parsimony, but is not normed to any scale. A lower value indicates a better fit, but there is no guide to determine how low is low enough, and it must be used in comparison to AIC values from other models. AIC determines model parsimony by subtracting a penalizing factor equal to the number of free parameters in the model from the maximum of the likelihood of the data obtained under that model: **AIC = -2 log *L* + 2p**

5. ***Bayesian Information Criterion*** (BIC: Weakliem, 1999) is a way to estimate the best model using only an in-sample estimate that is based on the maximization of a log likelihood function. The BIC also provides a measure of the posterior probability of each model for assessment purposes: **BIC = -2 log *L* + *p* log *N*.** This is also re-estimated to adjust for sample size, which provides an Adjusted BIC score.

6. ***Entropy*** (Muthén et al., 2002) is a summary statistic that is available to assess classification quality, with values ranging from 0 to 1. A value of one characterizes perfect classification ability, with lower numbers representing decreasing capacity to distinguish group membership

7. ***Lo-Mendell-Rubin Test*** (LMRT: Lo, Mendell, & Rubin, 2001) was designed to derive the correct distribution to test the difference between the k and k-1 class models. This distribution supplies a p-value that indicates whether the k model is a better fit than the k-1. A p-value of less than .05 represents a statistically significantly better fit. For a full description of the formulas, see Lo, Mendell, and Rubin's 2001 article in Biometrika.

8. ***Bootstrap Likelihood Difference Test*** (BLRT: McLachlan & Peel, 2000; Nylund, Asparouhov, & Muthén, 2006) also estimates the k and k-1 models to provide the likelihood for calculating the -2 x log likelihood difference. It creates a k-1 class model to generate a bootstrap sample and repeats this procedure multiple times (more times if there is a small difference between the models) to estimate the true distribution of the -2 x log likelihood difference. See McLachlan and Peel's 2000 book on a more detailed description of how to derive the test value.

After the shape of the general curve, or one class model, was established, multiple group models were run. Nylund et al. (2007) recommends examining a wide variety of statistical criteria in order to select a model: the fit statistics, model parsimony, estimation problems (such as model non-convergence, negative variances, model non-identification, etc.), meaningfulness of class prevalence, level of discrimination between classes (entropy), and the theoretical fit of trajectories.

For all of the following analyses the time points were fixed incrementally based on the timing of their administration: fall of first grade was fixed at 1, spring of first grade was fixed at 1.5, spring of second grade was fixed at 2.5., etc. As suggested by Muthén and Muthén (1998-2004), each of the analyses used automated multiple starting values in the optimization in order to reduce the probability that the solutions are based on local rather than global optima.

Each of the models in this chapter was estimated allowing for the residual variance between the fall and the spring semesters to correlate because the same teacher provided scores at both of these time points. The main difference between these models was the constraints on the variance structures of the latent growth factors (intercept, slope, and quadratic) between the groups. They are compared in the following sections and the model that best fit the data was selected for further examination.

SINGLE GROUP GROWTH MODEL

General Growth Using the Entire Sample

When all of the subjects are entered into the most restrictive model, a single class growth model which ignores intervention condition, a model that includes an intercept, slope, and quadratic growth factors captured the developmental trajectories best. On average, the subjects began first grade with a delinquency rating of 1.62 (SE=.78), which increased by .065 (SE=.17) each year, and decreased by -.006 (SE=.00) for each year squared. Overall, teacher ratings of delinquency increase with age, but the rate of the increase slows with age.

Table 15. Model Comparisons for Single Group Growth Model with all Conditions Combined

Model	Model Fit (df)	TLI	CFI	RM SEA	Prob	AIC	BIC	Adjust BIC
1.								
i	682.4 (64)	.74	.70	.12	.001	11260.1	11318.8	11277.6
2.								
i & s	394.3 (61)	.74	.70	.12	.001	10978.0	11050.3	10999.5
3.								
i, s, & q	183.5 (57)	.94	.94	.057	.075	10775.1	10865.5	10802.0

Ratio Tests	Model 1 vs. Model 2 288.12(3)**	Model 1 vs. Model 3 498.96(6)**	Model 2 vs. Model 3 210.84(3)**

** *Significant at the p<.001 level*

Examining the best fit model was instructive in several ways. It became apparent that classroom displays of aggressive and disruptive behavior, were relatively stable across time and peak in either late elementary or early middle school, and appear to be a low base rate behavior. It is important to note that even at its peak, classroom displays of aggressive and disruptive behavior are low and never rise above 2, which corresponds to "almost never" display of the constellation of aggressive and disruptive behavior. Examining the observed delinquency ratings and the modeled expected growth curve is also valuable. The model appeared to be better at predicting more distal outcomes than it was with the proximal measures of delinquency, which could be due to the missing time periods, grades 4 and 5. If the model correctly predicted developmental trajectories of delinquency, it appears the missing data collection points may be where the subjects display some of their highest levels of aggression; and therefore, very important information that could enable better predictions of the course of the developmental trajectories could be missing. Also, missing data from study drop-out could be seriously biasing the observed and/or estimated means and growth parameters.

Figure 8. **General Growth Model**

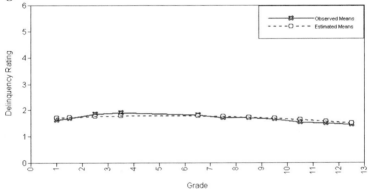

General Growth Model by Intervention Condition

When examining the growth curves by intervention status, it is evident that an intercept, slope, and quadratic latent growth factor are necessary to model the trajectories. However, modeling the different conditions separately does not result in a significantly better model fit than ignoring intervention status when modeling the growth curve.[5] This provides evidence that the intercepts, slopes, and class proportions do not differ significantly by intervention condition.

---

[5] Likelihood test: $\chi^2(144)=133.44$, p=.73

Inspecting the visual representation of the growth curves by intervention status confirms this finding,. The control classroom students had a lower mean aggression rating in the beginning of the study period; however, their scores increased more than their counterparts in the two intervention conditions. This difference can be detected when blowing up the graph, but the difference is not statistically significant, and therefore, condition will not be modeled in the following analyses. Examining the parameters by intervention status also provides more evidence that the growth models do not differ significantly.

Table 16. *Model Comparisons for Single Group Growth Model by Intervention Condition*

Model	Model Fit (df)	TLI	CFI	RMSEA	AIC	BIC	Adj. BIC
1. I	951.8 (192)	.70	.65	.13	11263.2	11439.4	11315.6
2. i & s	634.9 (183)	.81	.79	.105	10964.3	11181.2	11028.8
3. i, s, & q	392.9 (171)	.90	.90	.076	10746.3	11017.4	10826.9

Ratio Tests	Model 1 vs. Model 2	Model 1 vs. Model 3	Model 2 vs. Model 3
	316.89 (9)**	558.91 (21)**	242.02 (12)**

** $p < .001$

As modeling growth curves by intervention status did not increase model fit, it did not increase the accuracy of the model. In addition, the interventions were randomized using schools as blocking factors; and therefore, there is little reason to believe that there would be different proportions of subpopulations that make up the latent classes by intervention condition. Due to the fact that there did not appear to be any differences in the growth factors between the intervention conditions, that subjects were randomly assigned to conditions, and that the intervention lasted for only one year, they will not be included in the following group-based models. This greatly increases the power and model parsimony, as well as allow for the estimation of more complex models.

Figure 9. Growth Curves by Intervention Status

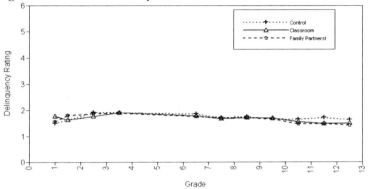

Table 17. Comparison of Parameters by Intervention Condition

Parameter	Control Group		GBG Group		FSP Group	
	Estimate	SE	Estimate	SE	Estimate	SE
Z_0	1.53	.06	1.68	.07	1.61	.06
Z_1	.08	.02	.05	.02	.07	.02
Z_2	-.006	.001	-.005	.001	-.007	.001
$V(\zeta_0)$	.46	.08	.86	.12	.50	.07
$V(\zeta_1)$	.02	.006	.04	.008	.03	.006
$V(\zeta_2)$	.00	.00	.00	.00	.00	.00
$V(\varepsilon_{1F})$	.32	.05	30	.05	.22	.04
$V(\varepsilon_{1S})$	.33	.04	.28	.04	.32	.04
$V(\varepsilon_{2S})$	.56	.07	.54	.06	.65	.07
$V(\varepsilon_{3S})$	.58	.07	.62	.07	.52	.06
$V(\varepsilon_{6S})$	.33	.04	.27	.03	.28	.04
$V(\varepsilon_{7S})$	.20	.03	.20	.03	.22	.03
$V(\varepsilon_{8S})$	.15	.02	.17	.02	.24	.03
$V(\varepsilon_{9S})$	.21	.03	.30	.04	.18	.02
$V(\varepsilon_{10S})$	.17	.02	.19	.03	.17	.02
$V(\varepsilon_{11S})$	.21	.03	.14	.02	.12	.02
$V(\varepsilon_{12S})$	.14	.03	.20	.03	.08	.02

ζ is the latent growth parameters, V is a variance, C is a covariance, and ε is the error term of the observed variable

GROUP-BASED TRAJECTORY MODELS

Group-Based Trajectory Models (also known as growth mixture models or GMM) are an extension of two statistical methodologies, multi-level modeling and group-based approaches. This methodology divides individuals into unobserved groups of similar developmental trajectories to examine group differences in growth. The purpose of the trajectory groups is to summarize the behaviors of a set of individuals; and therefore, individuals may or may not follow the overall pattern of the group to which they were assigned. Individual trajectory group members will most likely not follow their overall group patterns, just like with any other statistical summary.

Choosing the best fitting model is one of the most challenging aspects of group based trajectory modeling, as there are many different ways to specify the models and no way to directly test across non-nested models. Models with different numbers of latent classes are not nested, and therefore a number of statistical indicators must be used to pick the optimal solution, including the AIC, BIC, SSA BIC (the Baysian Information Criterion adjusted for sample size), Entropy, LVMR LRT (Lo-Mendell-Rubin Test) and Adjusted LMR LRT (Bootstrap Likelihood Difference Test). Five different ways of modeling variation in the latent growth factors were explored and tested against each other in the following sections.

As this is a relatively new technique, there is some concern about the theoretical assumptions, in particular the true existence of a set number of distinct developmental trajectories and whether people can actually be classified into these trajectories. Even if experts can agree on the existence of distinct trajectories, there is still a debate about whether the modeling approach should allow for variation the trajectories (Kreuter & Muthén, 2007; 2008; Raudenbush, 2005; Sampson & Laub, 2005). There are many different ways in which to define the variance and covariance structures of the latent growth factors that define how closely group members follow the overall pattern. These variance structures provide slightly different results (both theoretically and empirically) and ways in which to define group membership.

The different ways in which to model variation around trajectories will be examined. In this section five different variance/covariance structures are explored: (1) not allowing any variation in the intercept or slope factor, (2) freeing the variance of the intercept and slope, but constraining them to be equal across classes, (3) allowing the variance of the intercept to differ between class, but constraining the slope variance to be equal across class, (4) allowing variance in the slope factor to differ across class, but imposing equality of variance between classes on the intercept factor, and (5) permitting the variance of the intercept and the slope growth factors to differ across class. The differences in parameter estimation due to different variance assumptions will be discussed in the next chapter.

As with the general one class growth model, the residual error variances of the two measurements in first grade are allowed to covary because they were provided by the same teachers. In addition to this model specification, the variance in the quadratic term were fixed to zero because the variance was too small to estimate for each of the following models. Therefore, each model and each class within each model have no variance in their quadratic growth factor. This model constraint means that each individual within a group had the same quadratic growth curve because there is so little variation between individuals in a group in this term that it was too small to estimate.

No Variance in Growth Factors

The first method of group-based trajectory modeling that was explored is the model described by Nagin (2005) and is the most restricted model. This method does not allow for variation in the latent growth factors within or across classes. The growth model was run using one through eight classes and each model's fit indices are summarized in the table below. The four class model was selected as the model of best fit because most of the fit indices (AIC, BIC, and SSA BIC) leveled off at this point. The entropy was also quite high in this model (.87) and the LVMR was significant for this condition and not the five group model. The only indicator that designates that more classes were necessary to model the data is the Bootstrap Likelihood Test. According to Nylund (2006), all the fit indices need to be considered, and therefore, the 4 class model will be selected over the other models.

In this 4 class model, there are four distinct trajectories with different class proportions, intercepts and slopes. They were named using Moffitt's Taxonomy in mind, with names reflecting the trajectories they appeared to represent: (1) An Abstainer (AB) group made up of 64.0% of the sample (N=451), (2) A High Declining Group (HDG) group made up of 6.8% of the sample (N=49), (3) A High

Adolescent-Limited (ALH) group also made up of 6.8% of the sample (N= 44), and (4) A Low Adolescent-Limited (ALL) group made up of 22.3% of the sample (N=134). By design, none of the latent growth factors have any variance within their groups. The AB group has an initial rating of 1.37 (SE=.04), slope of .03 (SE=.01), and quadratic of -.003 (SE=.001). The HDG group, a small group, began much higher, with a mean intercept of 3.98 (SE=.19), a negative slope of -.308 (SE=.07), and a positive quadratic term of .009 (SE=.005). The ALH, another small group, began in the middle of the other two groups in delinquency ratings, with an initial rating of 2.16 (SE=.27), positive slope of .35 (SE.09), and negative quadratic term of -.027 (SE=.007). The final group, ALL, began with a relatively low intercept of 1.52 (SE=.07), a positive slope of .20, and a negative quadratic term of -.014 (SE=.002).

Table 18. Model Comparisons with No Variance in Growth Factors

	AIC	BIC	SSA BIC	Entropy	LVMR LRT p-value	BLRT
1	10775.1	10865.5	10802.0	1.00		
2	11004.2	11090.1	11029.7	.87	1367.00,p<.001	1419.40,p<.001
3	10678.2	10782.1	10709.1	.85	321.70, p=.005	334.03,p<.001
4	**10466.9**	**10588.9**	**10503.2**	**.87**	**211.20,p=.014**	**219.30, P<.001**
5	10387.4	10527.5	10429.0	.81	84.28, p=.34	87.51, p<.001
6	10309.9	10468.1	10356.9	.83	82.32, p=.20	85.48,p<.001
7	10268.2	10444.4	10320.6	.83	47.88, p=.57	49.72,p<.001
8	10234.3	10428.6	10292.1	.84	39.17, p=1.0	40.68,p<.001

Basically, the AB group, which made up the majority of the sample, started low and their scores remained stable over the study period. The HDG group started the highest, but was the only group with a negative slope, and ended with lower ratings of delinquencies than either of the AL groups. The ALH group started higher than the ALL group, and also increased aggression at an elevated rate compared to the ALL group.

Figure 10. *Growth Trajectories by Class with No Variance in Latent Growth Factors*

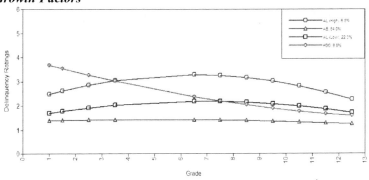

Model 1. Allowing Variance in the Intercept and Slope Factor

When allowing heterogeneity in the intercept and slope factors, generally fewer numbers of latent classes are needed to capture the different growth trajectories. This also makes for a less parsimonious model because a more complex set of parameters are needed to model variation around the latent growth factors. In this first set of models, the variance between the latent classes will be constrained to be equal because this is the most restricted and parsimonious model that allows variance. A three class model appears to be the optimal solution when considering all the fit indices:

1. When moving from the four to the three class model, the AIC, BIC, and SSA BIC do not drop as considerably.
2. The entropy is still relatively high (.89).
3. The Lo-Mendell-Rubin and Bootstrap Likelihood Difference Test were both significant for the three class model. This indicates that a three class model is a significantly better fit than a two class model, and there is no significant difference between the three and four class models, according to the Lo-Mendell-Rubin. The Bootstrap Likelihood Difference Test remained significant for all the models examined.

The three groups have different class proportions, intercepts, and slopes. The Adolescent-Limited group (AL) is made up of 9.3% of the sample (N=53), the High Declining Group (HDG) is comprised of 10.1% (N=68), and the Abstainer group (AB) is made up of the majority of the sample, 80.7% of the sample (N=557). AB has an initial mean aggression rating of 1.22 (SE=.15), HDG has a baseline average score of 3.85 (SE=.17), and AL has a 1.36 (SE=.04) mean aggression rating in the fall of first grade. The slope and quadratic terms also differed by class: AL has a mean slope of .55 and quadratic of -.042, HDG has a mean slope of -.312 and quadratic of .012, and AB has a mean slope of .063 and quadratic of -.005.

Table 19. Model Comparison Allowing Equal Variance in Latent Growth Factors

	AIC	BIC	SSA BIC	Entropy	LVMR LRT p-value	BLRT
1	10812.41	10893.76	10893.78	1.0		
2	10610.74	10710.16	10610.31	.82	207.9,p<.01	209.674,p<.01
3	**10394.99**	**10512.49**	**10429.93**	**.89**	**215.5, p<.01**	**223.746,p<.01**
4	10342.89	10478.46	10383.21	.86	57.88, p=.66	60.100, p<.001
5	10301.93	10455.58	10347.62	.83	67.35, p=.31	69.942, p<.001
6	10216.95	10388.68	10268.03	.90	47.26, p=.10	49.068,p<.001

Figure 11. Growth Trajectories by Class with Equal Variance in Latent Growth Factors

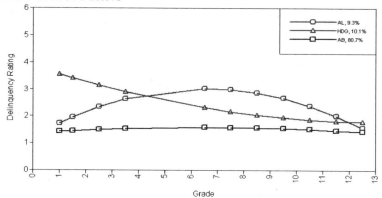

Basically, AL and AB both had lower initial ratings of delinquency, their ratings increased with age, but this increase decreased with time. The main difference between the two groups was the size of the slope term, with the slope of AL being about nine times greater than the slope in AB. The most noteworthy difference between classes is the intercept in AB is much higher than AL or LCP, and direction of the slope factor in HDG is negative. AB represents a growth trajectory that begins high and decreases with age, but this decrease lessens with age.

Model 2. Allowing Unequal Variance in the Intercept but not the Slope Factor

The next model loosens the variance restrictions on the intercept but not the slope factor. This will be a more complex model because it allows the intercepts between the different classes to have different variances – one class may be comprised of a relatively homogeneous group of individuals in respect to their initial aggression ratings where another class can be made up of a relatively heterogeneous group of individuals. Once again, a three class model appears to be the optimal solution when considering all the fit indices:

1. When moving from the three to the four class model, the AIC, BIC, and SSA do not drop as considerably.
2. The entropy is still relatively high (.80).
3. The Lo-Mendell-Rubin and Bootstrap Likelihood Difference Test were both significant for the three class model, but the Lo-Mendell-Rubin was not significant for a four class model.

The three groups have different class proportions, intercepts, and slopes and show a better split in groups that when constraining the variance to be equal. HDG is made up of 11.2% of the sample (N=73), AB is comprised of 66.4% (N=475), and AL is made up of the remaining 22.4% of the sample (N=130). HDG has an initial mean aggression rating of 3.71 (SE=.25), AB has a baseline average score of 1.32 (SE=.05), and AL has a 1.36 (SE=.12) mean aggression rating in the fall of first grade. The slope and quadratic terms also differed by class: HDG has a mean slope of -.302 (SE=.06) and quadratic of .012 (SE=.004), AB has a mean slope of .047 (SE=.01) and quadratic of -

.004 (SE=.001) and AL has a mean slope of .320 (SE=.06) and quadratic of -.022 (SE=.004).

Table 20. Group-Based Model Comparisons Allowing Variance in Intercept Only

	AIC	BIC	SSA BIC	Entropy	LVMR LRT p-value	BLRT
1	10812.4	10893.8	10893.8	1.0		
2	10560.3	10664.3	10591.2	.58	254.30,p<.001	262.10,p<.001
3	**10341.8**	**10463.8**	**10378.1**	**.80**	**218.12,p=.04**	**226.49,p<.001**
4	10257.3	10397.4	10299.0	.78	89.08,p=.52	92.49,p<.001
5	10163.4	10321.6	10210.4	.81	86.61,p=.53	89.9,p=.07
6	10084.9	10261.1	10137.3	.83	42.33,p=.61	43.96, p=1.0

The most significant differences between all of the three classes are: (1) the intercept in HDG is much higher than AB or AL, and (2) the direction of the slope factor in HDG is negative. HDG represents a growth trajectory that begins high and decreases with age, but this decrease lessens with age. The two groups which more closely resembled each other are the AB and X groups. Abstainers and AL both had lower initial ratings of delinquency, their ratings increased with age, but this increase slowed with time. The paramount difference between these two groups was the size of the slope term, with the slope of AL being about seven times greater than the slope in AB.

Figure 12. Growth Trajectories by Class Allowing Unequal Variance in Intercept Only

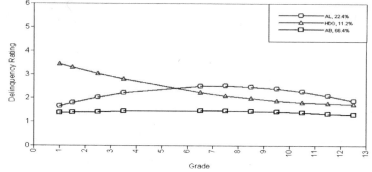

In this model, the variance in the latent intercept factor was allowed to vary between groups. LCP and AL have a much higher variation in their intercept factors than AB (.261 vs. .101). There is 2.5 times more variation in the intercept factors in HDG and AL groups than in AB, meaning that members of these two groups are more heterogeneous in respect to their baseline delinquency ratings than members of the AB group.

Model 3. Allowing Unequal Variance in Slope but not the Intercept Factor

The following model loosens the variance restrictions on the slope but not the intercept factor. This model is more complex model as it allows the slopes between the different classes to have different variances – one class may be comprised of a relatively homogeneous group of individuals in respect to the development of their aggression ratings over time while another class can be made up of a relatively heterogeneous group of individuals. Once again, a three class model was the optimal solution when considering all the fit indices:

1. When moving from the three to the four class model, the AIC, BIC, and SSA do not drop as considerably.
2. The entropy is the highest in the three class model (.80).
3. The Lo-Mendell-Rubin the Likelihood Difference Test was significant for the three class model and not the four class model. This indicates that a three class model is a better fit than a two class model, but there is no significant difference between the three and four class models.

The three groups have different class proportions, intercepts, and slopes. AL is made up of 22.2% of the sample (N=127), HDG is comprised of 10.0% (N=68), and AB is made up of the remaining 67.8% of the sample (N=483). AB has an initial mean aggression rating of 1.34 (SE=.10), HDG has a baseline average score of 3.87 (SE=.17), and AL has a 1.35 (SE=.04) mean aggression rating in the fall of first grade. The slope and quadratic terms also differed by class: AL has a mean slope of .32 (SE=.05) and quadratic of -.02 (SE=.004), HDG has a mean slope of -.33 (SE=.05) and quadratic of .01 (SE=.003), and AB has a mean slope of .042 (SE=.009) and quadratic of -.004 (SE=.001). AL and AB both had lower initial ratings of delinquency and their ratings increased with age, but this increase decreased with time.

Table 21. Group-Based Model Comparisons Allowing Variance in Slope Only

	AIC	BIC	SSA BIC	Entropy	LVMR LRT p-value	BLRT
1	10812.4	10893.8	10893.8	1.0		
2	10545.9	10649.8	10576.8	.66	268.28,p<.001	276.51, p<.001
3	**10314.9**	**10436.9**	**10351.1**	**.80**	**230.22,p=.003**	**239.05, p<.001**
4	10215.5	10355.6	10257.2	.72	103.36,p=.12	107.32, p<.01
5	10158.1	10316.3	10205.1	.76	101.07,p=.09	104.95,p<.001
6	10132.8	10309.1	10185.3	.77	37.52,p=.09	38.96, p=.030

Figure 13. Growth Trajectories with Unequal Variance in Slope Only

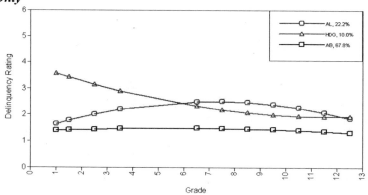

In this model, the variance in the latent slope factor was allowed to vary between groups. AL and HDG have equal variance in their slope factors (.003), while AB has a smaller variance (.001). AL and HDG have three times greater variation in their slope factors than AB.

Model 5. **Allowing Unequal Variance in the Intercept and Slope Factor**

The final model relaxed the variance restrictions even further by allowing the variance in both the intercept and the slope factors to differ by class. This model is the most complex model with regard to the latent growth factors' variance structures. It allows the intercepts and slopes between the different classes to have different variances so that one class may be comprised of a relatively homogeneous group of individuals with respect to their initial aggression ratings and slopes where another class can be made up of a relatively heterogeneous group of individuals. Under these less restricted variance assumptions, a three class model again appears to be the optimal solution when considering all the fit indices:

1. When moving from the three to four class model, the AIC, BIC, and SSA do not drop as considerably.
2. The entropy is still relatively high (.78).
3. The Lo-Mendell-Rubin Likelihood Difference Test was significant for the three class but not the four class model. This indicates that a three class model is a significantly better fit than a two-class model, but there is no significant difference between the three and four class models.

Table 22. *Group-Based Model Comparisons Allowing Variance in Intercept and Slope*

	AIC	BIC	SSA BIC	Entropy	LVMR LRT p-value	BLRT
1	10812.4	10893.8	10893.8	1.0		
2	10538.1	10646.6	10570.4	.60	279.1,p<.01	276.51,p<.001
3	**10294.0**	**10420.6**	**10331.7**	**.78**	**242.8,p<.01**	**252.10,p<.001**
4	10204.2	10348.8	12247.2	.72	94.3,p=.15	97.89, p<.001
5	10125.3	10288.0	10173.7	.77	83.7,p=.46	88.06, p<.001
6	10034.7	10214.8	10087.8	.82	86.7,p=.12	45.30, p=.43

The three groups have different class proportions, intercepts, and slopes. HDG is made up of 11.1% of the sample (N=75), AB is comprised of 64.5% (N=466), and AL is made up of the remaining

24.4% of the sample (N=137). HDG has an initial mean aggression rating of 3.76 (SE=.21), AB has a baseline average score of 1.31 (SE=.05), and AL has a 1.37 (SE=.10) mean aggression rating in the fall of first grade. The slope and quadratic terms also differed by class: HDG has a mean slope of -.314 (SE=.05) and quadratic of .013 (SE=.003), AB has a mean slope of .044 (SE=.05) and quadratic of -.004 (SE=.001), and AL has a mean slope of .302 (SE=.05) and quadratic of -.021 (SE=.004).

The most striking difference between the three classes is that the HDG group starts out much higher on the delinquency scale than either the AB or AL groups and that direction of the slope factor in HDG is negative instead of positive. HDG represents a growth trajectory that begins high and decreases with age, but this effect decreases with age. In essence, AB and AL both had lower initial ratings of delinquency, their ratings increased with age, while HDG had higher initial ratings of delinquency, and their ratings decreased with age. The main difference between the AB and AL groups was the size of the slope term, with the slope of AL being about seven times greater than the slope in AB.

Figure 14. Growth Trajectories by Class Allowing Unequal Variance in Intercept and Slope

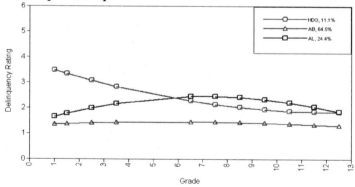

In this model, both the variance in the latent intercept and slope factors were allowed to vary between groups. HDG and AL have a standard deviation of their intercept factors that is 1.5 greater than that of AB (.19 vs. .081). There is far more variation in the intercept factors in HDG and AL than in AB, meaning that members of these two groups are more heterogeneous regarding their baseline delinquency ratings than members of AB. The differences in variation in the slope factors are much smaller, with AB having a variance of .002 in the latent slope factor and HDG and AL having slope variation that is less than .001. The AB group has very little variance, meaning that they are a very homogeneous group that begin with a low initial aggression score and remain low through the study period. Both the HDG and AL groups are more heterogeneous and have more variability in their group members than the AB group.

SUMMARY

This chapter explored whether group-based trajectory modeling is a better method of capturing delinquency growth curves than traditional single group modeling. It also investigated the different ways in which the group-based models could be defined and how changes in model restrictions impacted the final model. The different model constraints produced slightly different growth curves, number of trajectory groups, and class proportions.

The first important finding was that a general growth model found that ratings of aggressive/disruptive behavior in the classroom are extremely stable across time. Overall, the sample displayed very low levels of aggressive/disruptive behavior and it appears to peak in late elementary or early middle school. The possibility that growth curves differed by intervention status was also tested and found to be insignificant.

After the general group model was established, a series of group-based trajectory models using five approaches were assessed, each differing on exactly how a "group" is defined. As group-based trajectory modeling is a relatively new technique, there are still unanswered theoretical and methodological questions about the meaning of trajectory groups and their membership. As the purpose of the groups is to summarize the behaviors of a set of individuals, the degree of heterogeneity in a group becomes a key issue. Some researchers believe that a group must constitute a relatively homogeneous population within a heterogeneous population (Nagin, 2005), while others believe that smaller heterogeneous populations make up the larger heterogeneous population (Fuzhong, Duncan, Duncan, & Acock, 2001; Muthén, 2000; Schafer et al., 2003). As this is a relatively new technique, there is some concern about the theoretical assumptions, in particular the true existence of a set number of distinct developmental trajectories, and if people can actually be classified into these trajectories. Even if experts can agree on the existence of distinct trajectories, there is still a debate about whether the modeling approach should allow for variation the trajectories (Kreuter & Muthén, 2007; 2008; Raudenbush, 2005; Sampson & Laub, 2005). There are many different ways in which to define the variance and covariance structures of the latent growth factors that define how closely group members follow the overall pattern. These variance structures provide slightly different results (both theoretically and empirically) and ways in which to define group membership. This study took an empirical approach to the question of how within- and between-group heterogeneity should be defined.

Five different definitions of a "group" were tested; from the strictest characterization which restricted groups to be as homogeneous as possible, to the loosest definition that allowed group members to vary a great deal in their trajectories: (1) not allowing any variation in the intercept or slope factor, (2) freeing the variance of the intercept and slope, but constraining them to be equal across classes, (3) allowing the variance of the intercept to differ between class, but constraining the slope variance to be equal across class, (4) allowing variance in the slope factor to differ across class, but imposing equality of variance between classes on the intercept factor, and (5) permitting the variance of the intercept and the slope growth factors to differ across class.

Each of the five approaches required the estimation of between six and eight different models for model selection, as described by Nylund (2006). The first, and most restrictive, approach found four groups, best described as: (1) an abstainer group, (2) a high but declining group, (3) a low adolescence-limited group, and (4) a high adolescence-limited group. The remainder of the approaches established three group models that showed only a few minor differences. Each of the approaches found three groups, which are best described as: (1) an abstainer group (AB), (2) an adolescence-limited group (AL), and (3) a high declining group (HDG). The different approaches that allowed variation produced models with statistically equivalent parameters, with the only major difference being in the class proportions. The model in which the variance in all the latent factors was fixed to be equal (the second most restrictive model) produced different class proportions than the other models that allowed for variance invariance across the latent growth factors.

Modeling in the variation allows diversity between the group members, and the questions become how heterogeneous is the group and does group membership still have any meaning. By constraining the variance to be equal between groups, or requiring variance invariance, each of the groups will be as heterogeneous as the others. Group members will be allowed to vary around the group mean intercept and slope, but the variation within the groups will be equal. Under these variance assumptions, it only took three groups to fit the data. Allowing the individuals to vary around their group averages, it eliminated the need for an additional trajectory group. The change in assumptions both increased and reduced the complexity of the model.

The most important lesson that came out of comparing the different variance assumptions was that once variance was allowed within groups, a three class model was always the best fit. This supports the conclusion that a three class model is a reliable finding and not simply an artifact of how the latent variances are defined. Another important finding was that once variance was allowed to be estimated separately within group in either or both the latent constructs, the parameter estimates were statistically equivalent. The same results were produced when the intercept variance, slope variance, or intercept and slope variance were freed to vary between classes. These estimates were slightly different from those from the model in which the variance of both parameters were fixed to be equal. The next chapter will explore the differences between the models and make an argument as to which model best fits the data that is both theoretically and empirically meaningful.

Which Model Fits Best?

This chapter focuses on selecting which of the previous models best fits both Moffitt's theory and the data. The meaning of the estimation of variance in the latent growth factors is examined and compared as each of the different combinations of freed and fixed variances has different implications for the meaning of the group and the heterogeneity of the individuals that make up that group.

With the fundamental issue of the validity and reliability of trajectory group membership at the center of a current dispute (see ANNALS of the American Academy of Political and Social Science Issue 602, November 2005, which was devoted to life-course theory and the legitimacy of group-based trajectory modeling), the different variance structures of the latent classes become more important in this debate. The following section attempts to provide some clarity on the issues under dispute and provide empirical evidence to respond to some of the questions.

These different variance structures have implications beyond the empirical changes; they alter the theoretical definition of a group by specifying how similar group members are with respect to their developmental trajectories. Three definitions discussed in this book included: (Model 1) total group homogeneity, (Model 2) group heterogeneity that is the same in each class, and (Models 3 through 5) group heterogeneity that varies by class.

For the no variance restriction (Model 1), a latent class is a collection of individuals who follow the same pattern, with only random error producing differences in the trajectories of group members. In other words, group membership alone (along with their theoretical predictors) is the only factor driving trajectories. While no one would claim that each member of the trajectory group will follow their group flawlessly, theoretically the zero variance method will produce group members that are as similar as possible (Nagin, 2005).

If that theoretical assumption is modified and group members are allowed to vary from one another along a distribution, groups approximate smaller heterogeneous sub-populations. A group now estimates heterogeneity, so the next question becomes, how much heterogeneity should be allowed? Should each group be equally heterogeneous, or would each have its own amount of variation? While it might seem like restricting variance within each group to be equal would be an artificial assumption (Model 2), if there is no clear theoretical reason to allow variance to be estimated for each group separately, it would make sense to make them equal both for the sake of parsimony and the fact that freeing this parameter could leave the model vulnerable for overestimation. This simply illustrates how a seemingly minor modeling specification can significantly alter the empirical findings. The question of freeing additional parameters for estimation gets very tricky as the estimation technique is retrospective and data-driven, and consequently, the more parameters freed, the more likely the findings could be based on data artifacts.

In addition to concerns about potential data mining pitfalls, if group members are now heterogeneous, what makes them a group? How does this alter the meaning of this group? These questions should be addressed depending on the theory that is being tested and/or the purpose of deriving the groups, but there is currently little to no guidance to guide criminologists in this regard.

Moffitt's theory (1993) does not expressly address the issue of variability; however, some of her hypotheses allude to the type of heterogeneity that would be expected in the groups. Moffitt describes a group of abstainers (AB). These individuals never engage in delinquent behavior and therefore the group should be relatively or entirely homogeneous. Her next group, the adolescence-limited offenders (AL), shifts in and out of delinquency due to a perceived disconnect between social and physical maturity along with deviant peer role models. Implicit in this statement is that there would be within group variability because each individual will have a different experience with the maturity gap and level of exposure to deviant peers from whom they mimic the delinquent behavior. Finally, the life-course-persistent offenders (LCP) should exhibit antisocial behavior throughout the course of their lives and across their environmental domains. Her theory does not provide many hints as to how diverse this group would be expected to be.

Taken together, it seems logical that in order to test Moffitt's theory within group heterogeneity should be estimated separately for the AL and LCP groups because there is a good reason to believe that there will be a large amount of variation in the AL group. The AB group may not need any variation modeled at all. Empirically support was found for this deduction as one group was found to be more homogeneous than the others once variation is allowed to be estimated separately. The standard error of the intercept is half as large in Group 3 (the group that most closely resembles Moffitt's AB group), compared to the other groups, and the standard error of the slope in this group is too small to even be estimated. In other words, individuals who did not exhibit aggressive/disruptive behavior over the course of the study had more similar trajectories than those who either escalated (the group that approximates Moffitt's AL offenders) or deescalated in their behavior (the group that most closely follows Moffitt's hypothesized trajectory for LCP offenders).

Theoretically it sense that groups that change in their displays of antisocial behavior over time would be more heterogeneous because there is the potential for many theoretically-relevant time-varying and time-invariant factors could influence the intercept and slope of an individual's trajectory. In accordance with Moffitt's theory, factors such as exposure to deviant peers and experiences with the maturity gap may influence their individual trajectories in addition to predicting their group membership in the AL group. For the LCP offenders, individual differences, either in their environmental and psych-physiological dysfunction, or other constructs that may vary over time and influence their trajectories as they change. Additionally, it is possible that an entirely different group of variables that is influencing with in group variation.

COMPARING MODELS

When comparing across the different variance assumptions, the models estimate very similar parameters. Using a three class model and only changing the variance restrictions developed in the previous chapter, Model 2, which was the most restrictive, estimated parameters that were slightly different than Models 3 through 5, which were all statistically equivalent. Since all of these models were nested, it is possible to test across them to see which one fits the data best using a Likelihood ratio test.[6] Models 3, 4, and 5 were all better model fits than Model 2.[7] Model 5 was also a better fit than either Model 3 or

---

[6] Likelihood ratio test, normed on a Chi-Square distribution:
$\chi^2(df_{null}-df_{alt})=(-2)(LL_{null} - LL_{alt})$
[7] Likelihood ratio: $\chi^2(2)=55.18$, p<.0001, $\chi^2(2)=82.15$, p<.0001, and $\chi^2(4)=104.6$, p<.0001, respectively

Model 4.[8] Therefore, Model 5, which included unequal variances in the intercept and slope factors between the classes was the best empirical model.

Table 23. *Picking the Model of Best Fit*

	Model 2 Fixed i Fixed s	Model 3 Free i Fixed s	Model 4 Fixed i Free s	**Model 5 Free i Free s**
Entropy	.89	.80	.80	**.78**
AIC	10394.99	10341.82	10314.85	**10294.04**
BIC	10512.49	10463.84	10436.87	**10420.58**
SSA BIC	10429.93	10378.11	10351.14	**10331.67**
-2 LL	-5171.50	-5143.91	-5130.425	**-5119.20**
"Adolescent-Limited"				
Intercept mean	1.22 (.15)	1.36 (.12)	1.34 (.10)	**1.36 (.10)**
Intercept variance	*Fixed*	.26 (.04)	*Fixed*	**.19 (.03)**
Slope Mean	.55 (.07)	.32 (.06)	.32 (.05)	**.30 (.05)**
Slope Variance	*Fixed*	*Fixed*	.003 (.000)	**.002 (.000)**
Quadratic Mean	-.04 (.005)	-.02 (.004)	-.02 (.004)	**-.02 (.004)**
Quadratic Variance	*Fixed to 0*	*Fixed to 0*	*Fixed to 0*	***Fixed to 0***
Class Proportion	9.3%	22.4%	22.2%	**24.4%**
"High Declining Group"				
Intercept mean	3.85 (.17)	3.72 (.25)	3.87 (.17)	**3.67 (.21)**
Intercept variance	*Fixed*	.26 (.04)	*Fixed*	**.19 (.03)**
Slope Mean	-.31 (.05)	-.30 (.06)	-.33 (.05)	**-.32 (.05)**
Slope Variance	*Fixed*	*Fixed*	.003 (.000)	**.002 (.000)**
Quadratic Mean	.012 (.003)	.01 (.004)	.014 (.003)	**.013 (.003)**
Quadratic Variance	*Fixed to 0*	*Fixed to 0*	*Fixed to 0*	***Fixed to 0***
Class Proportion	10.0%	11.2%	10.0%	**11.1%**
"abstainer"				
Intercept mean	1.36 (.04)	1.32 (.50)	1.35 (.04)	**1.32 (.05)**
Intercept variance	*Fixed*	.10 (.03)	*Fixed*	**.08 (.03)**
Slope Mean	.06 (.01)	.05 (.01)	.042 (.009)	**.04 (.009)**
Slope Variance	*Fixed*	*Fixed*	.001 (.000)	**.000 (.000)**
Quadratic Mean	-.005 (.001)	-.004 (.001)	-.004 (.001)	**-.004 (.001)**
Quadratic Variance	*Fixed to 0*	*Fixed to 0*	*Fixed to 0*	***Fixed to 0***
Class Proportion	80.7%	66.4%	67.8/%	**64.5%**

---

[8] Likelihood ratio: $\chi^2(2)=49.42$, p<.0001 and $\chi^2(2)=22.45$, p<.0001.

While the models discussed in the previous chapter were based on different variance structures, there were many similarities between them in regards to class enumeration, latent growth factor parameterization, and class proportions. The first set of models restricted the variance of the latent growth parameters and therefore more groups were needed to capture the growth trajectories. However, when the variance of the latent terms is allowed to be estimated in various fashions, the results were strikingly similar. A three class model was always selected as the best-fitting model.

While the three class model was always the best fit, the individuals followed the overall group trajectory differently. For a visual representation of the way in which individuals follow their group trajectories, see the following figures. Each thin line represents an individual's unique trajectory[9] and the thick line characterizes the group average. Each of the following spaghetti plots include a random sample of individuals who would most likely be classified as HDG (which is the group that most closely resembles Moffitt's Life-Course-Persistent offenders) based on their observed delinquency trajectory. Each of the following plots look remarkably similar and it does not appear that changing the latent variance structure changes the variation in the individual trajectories in relationship to the group average. It also appears that the proportion of the number of people from the sample that belong to this group remains stable, regardless of how the variance in the latent growth factors are allowed to differ across group.

Changing the latent growth parameters variance restrictions appears to increase the amount of variation around the group mean for the AL group, see figures below. In fact, when models were allowed to estimate the variation around only the intercept factor separately, the AL group had twice as much variation around the intercept than when it was restricted to be equal. When the slope was allowed to vary, the slope term had a variation that was three times larger than when it was restricted. When they were both allowed to vary, the variance in the AL group's latent growth terms was at least two times greater, meaning that there was a greater difference between the individuals in the AL group when the model allowed these differences to be estimated. When more variation was allowed, a greater number of individuals were assigned to the AL class – the class proportion doubles, from 9.3% to between 22.4% and 24.4%.

---

[9] Individuals assigned to their most likely class

Figure 15. *Spaghetti Plots of High Declining Group*

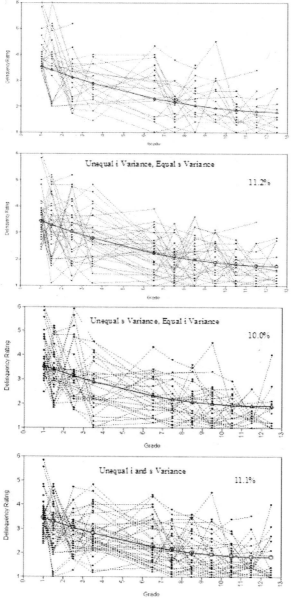

Figure 16. Spaghetti Plot of Adolescent-Limited Offenders

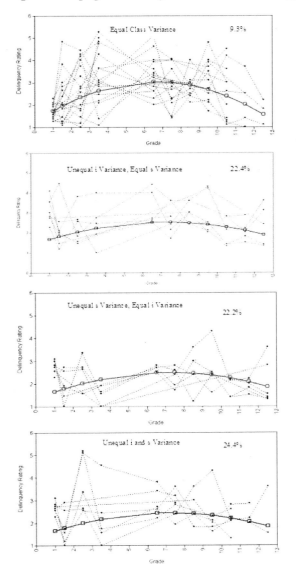

The differences in the AB group when estimating the latent variance parameters were striking. The amount of variation around the group mean trajectory as greatly diminished, as was the proportion of individuals assigned to the AB class. When allowing the variance of the intercept to differ by class, the variance decreased from .12 to .10; however, more interestingly, when allowing the slope variance to vary by class, it remained exactly the same. When allowing both the intercept and slope variance to differ between classes, the intercept variance and the slope variance were again reduced and the proportion of the sample assigned to the AB class was reduced. The individuals that made up the AB group now appeared to have much more homogeneous growth trajectories than the individuals in either the LCP or AL groups.

It appears that loosening the restrictions on the equality of the variance of the latent growth terms did significantly change the make up of the groups even if it did not have a huge impact on the class parameterizations. Through examining the plots it becomes evident that changing the restrictions made a discernable impact on the homogeneity of most of the groups.[10] In sum, the HDG group was not visibly affected by the changes in variance restrictions, but the other groups did experience changes. It appears that allowing variance differences across classes moves individuals from the AB group into the AL group. The plots also demonstrate that AB group is more homogeneous than either the AL or the HDG groups, and that by constraining the variation to be equal; their variances are inflated to simply reflect those of the larger AB group.

---

[10] As one group remained essentially unchangeable by imposing different variance structures, it raises the question of whether perhaps this is a unique grouping and the other two classes are simply artifacts one group that only differs by degree (meaning that AB and AL groups are both drawn from the same distribution). This hypothesis was tested, mimicking the unequal variance assumption, and found to be a worse fit: AIC=10623.08, BIC=10722.50, Adj.BIC=10652.65, Entropy=.92. Therefore, it appears that there are three discrete groups.

Figure 17. Spaghetti Plot of Abstainers

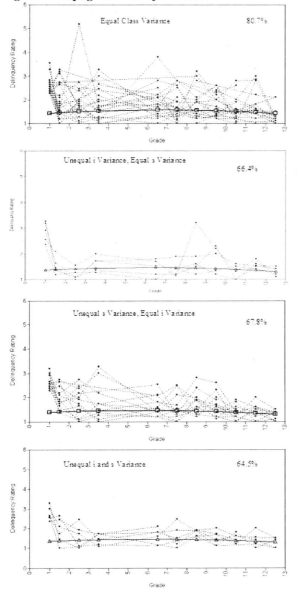

MODEL OF BEST FIT

After examining all the evidence, the three class model with unequal variation in both the intercept and the slope growth factors was selected as the best fitting model. This model was selected because:

1. The spaghetti plots demonstrated that some groups were more homogeneous than others when the variance restrictions were relaxed.
2. The likelihood ratio test offered empirical evidence that when the variance restrictions were loosened, the model fits better, even when penalizing for a less parsimonious model.
3. The differences in the parameter estimations changed from Model 2 to Models 3 through 5, but did not change appreciably between Models 3, 4, and 5.
4. There is no theoretical reason to believe that the variance in the growth factors would be equal across the groups.
5. There is no theoretical reason to believe that within group variation in either the intercepts or slopes would differ between classes while the other would remain invariant.

When examining how closely the model fits the data, it is instructive to look at the observed class growth trajectories and the estimated ones. From the graphic below, it appears that both the HDG and AL groups were predicted with more accuracy than the AB group. Interestingly, the AL group was the one that had greater variation, so it follows that this group would be the most difficult to capture; however, since the AB group had such a small amount of variance, it could be the most difficult to predict any significant proportion of the variation.

Under this set of variance restrictions, the groups overlap quite a bit at each data collection point. Plotting the group means with 95% confidence intervals shows that the abstainer group is much more homogeneous than the high declining group and the adolescence-limited group. The groups also entirely overlap after middle school. It is apparent that it would be impossible to assign any individual to a trajectory group based on their delinquency rating after elementary school when it is possible to distinguish between the HDG and the AB/AL groups. However, after the transition to middle school, it does not appear that there is any one time period that could differentiate the

AL and HDG group members based on their teacher-ratings on delinquency.

Figure 18. *Observed Verses Estimated Best Fitting Model*

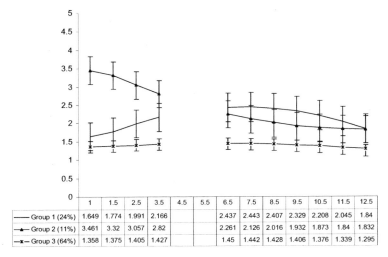

Figure 19. *Means and Confidence Intervals*

	1	1.5	2.5	3.5	4.5	5.5	6.5	7.5	8.5	9.5	10.5	11.5	12.5
Group 1 (24%)	1.649	1.774	1.991	2.166			2.437	2.443	2.407	2.329	2.208	2.045	1.84
Group 2 (11%)	3.461	3.32	3.057	2.82			2.261	2.126	2.016	1.932	1.873	1.84	1.832
Group 3 (64%)	1.358	1.375	1.405	1.427			1.45	1.442	1.428	1.406	1.376	1.339	1.295

Another important indication of how well the model fits is how well the latent growth factors capture the delinquency ratings at any one time point. It appears that the growth factors are relatively good at predicting delinquency ratings in the AL and HDG groups, (mean $R^2=.49$, SD=.17), but not as good at predicting scores at any one time point for the AB group (mean R^2=.11, SD=.06). This could be for a variety of reasons, including the fact that there are many more individuals in the AB group than the other groups, and the fact that the residuals between the three groups were specified to be equal. It is also possible that trying to model the deviations from such a low base-rate behavior, especially in this trajectory group, is beyond the ability of the model. In addition, the slope is so flat that there is more within time variance than between time variance in this group.[11] Due to this restriction, each deviation from the mean has relatively more influence than it would in another group.

Table 24. *R^2 for Each Observed Variable by Latent Class*

Observed Variable	Adolescent-Limited	High Decliner	Abstainer
First Grade Fall	.49	.49	.27
First Grade Spring	.36	.36	.17
Second Grade	.22	.22	.08
Third Grade	.23	.23	.08
Sixth Grade	.41	.41	.09
Seventh Grade	.52	.52	.10
Eighth Grade	.56	.56	.09
Ninth Grade	.55	.55	.07
Tenth Grade	.66	.66	.09
Eleventh Grade	.67	.67	.08
Twelfth Grade	.75	.75	.10

A final important issue to consider is the effect of missing data on the model. It does not appear that there is more data missing in any of the latent classes under these model specifications. It does not appear that missingness is related to latent class.

GROUP MEMBERS

As group members do not follow their trajectory groups flawlessly, especially when allowing variation among the latent growth factors,

---

[11] When examining the scatterplots of the observed verses expected delinquency scores, it is clear that the low R^2 is due to the fact that the model does not allow very much variation in the AB group.

another important part of selecting the best model is determining whether group membership appears to be meaningful and have external validity. This can be accomplished by creating profiles of the trajectory group members to characterize them. Once a model is selected, there are two methods through which to assign group membership to subjects in the study:

1. *Posterior Group-Membership Probabilities* are a set of probabilities that collectively calculate a specific individual's chances of belonging to each of the model trajectory groups. Together, these probabilities represent each subject's specific behavioral profile in respect to the trajectory classes. The posterior class probabilities of an individual i belonging to group j is calculated using Bayes's Theorem:

$$P(j \mid Y_i) = \frac{P(Y_i \mid j)\,\pi_i}{\Sigma\,P(Y_i \mid j)\,\pi_j}$$

2. *Pseudo Class Membership* uses a maximum-probability assignment to assign subjects to the class to which they have the highest posterior group-membership probability of membership (see Bandeen-Roche *et al.*, 1997). Pseudo class assignment is determined based on a random draw using the estimated conditional posterior probabilities of group membership, a set of probabilities that collectively calculate a specific individual's chance of belonging to each of the model trajectory groups (see Nagin, 2005).

There are pros and cons to using each of the methods of assigning individuals to groups. Using pseudo class membership is straight-forward and requires simple cross-tabulations. There are problems with this method and a major criticism is that it does not take into consideration that an individual's trajectory group membership is uncertain and based on a probability distribution. It also assumes equal weighting of each group member regardless of how likely it is that the individual belongs to each class. A more theoretical, but less intuitive method that uses the posterior class probabilities, addresses both of these concerns. Using the posterior class probabilities as weights, the uncertainty of group membership and the likelihood of an individual belonging to each of the groups is taken into account. These two methods simply approach the question of group membership in two theoretically and empirically different ways – either as an absolute (pseudo class membership) or as a probability distribution (posterior-group-membership probabilities).

Group Demographics

The following profiles of the groups are provided in both ways, the weighted averages using posterior class probabilities and the pseudo class membership. The weighted averages using posterior class probability uses the class probabilities as weights when calculating each of the groups' demographic profile. Each individual can contribute information for each group, depending on their posterior class probabilities. The average posterior class probability is computed by the following formula:

$$\overline{X}^{\,j} = (1/(N \times \pi_j)) \sum_{i=1}^{N} P\,(j\,|Y_i)\,x_i$$

There does not appear to be a large (or statistically significant) difference in the demographic profiles of the groups when using the pseudo class membership verses the posterior group-membership probability weighted average, which is likely a result of the model's relatively high entropy.

It is interesting to note that group assignment is quite different for males than for females. Very few females belong to the HDG group (5% of the females belong to the HDG group verses 16% of the males) and an overwhelming majority is part of the AB group (around 80% of females belong to this group compared to around 54% of the males). There are no significant differences in the racial make-up of the groups, nor was there any difference in the distribution of trajectory group by intervention status.

Family income and family type (number of primary caretakers) are not significantly different by trajectory group, although family type is approaching significance. It appears that abstainers more often come from a two-parent household, although this difference is not quite significant (p=.06).

Table 25. Group Demographics by Pseudo Class and Posterior Class Probability

	Adolescence-Limited		High Decliners		Abstainers		χ^2
	Pseudo N=164	Post Prob N=136	Pseudo Class N=75	Post Prob N=76	Pseudo N=438	Post Prob N=465	Across Class
Gender							
Male	27.4%	31.3%	16.3%	16.1%	56.2%	52.6%	56.22,
Female	11.7%	16.5%	5.4%	5.4%	82.9%	78.2%	p<.001
Race							
White	18.7%	22.0%	15.4%	15.4%	65.9%	62.6%	1.83, p=.40
Black	20.3%	24.6%	10.6%	10.4%	69.1%	65.0%	
Control	25.1%	28.8%	9.6%	9.1%	65.3%	62.1%	
Class	17.4%	21.4%	14.3%	14.0%	68.3%	64.6%	7.94, p=.09
Family	18.0%	22.9%	9.6%	14.1%	72.4%	67.4%	
Age							*ANOVA*
$F\ 1^{st}$	6.21	6.23	6.27	6.26	6.23	6.23	F(2,647)= .65, p=.52
Income							
<$5K	16.0%	15.0%	21.9%	20.6%	9.3%	11.9%	
$5K-	17.9%	16.9%	15.6%	17.0%	14.9%	15.5%	
$10K	19.8%	21.2%	21.9%	20.1%	20.3%	20.5%	20.85, p=.18
$20K	17.0%	17.2%	15.6%	16.6%	19.3%	18.4%	
$30K	16.0%	16.8%	14.1%	14.4%	22.5%	20.3%	
>$50K	2.8%	3.1%	7.8%	8.3%	5.1%	5.0%	
Family							
2 Par	38.1%	42.7%	36.5%	36.1%	53.6%	45.4%	12.13, p=.06
1 Par	53.6%	49.0%	53.8%	54.0%	39.9%	43.4%	

Group Members External Validity

A useful measure of external validity of group membership is how well trajectory group membership predicts other antisocial or delinquent behaviors. Moffitt made several hypotheses about how expressions of antisocial behavior should manifest by group. For instance, she hypothesizes that the AL group should be involved in more substance use because it symbolizes social maturity. Using posterior class probabilities, suspensions and tobacco, alcohol, and other drug use differences between the groups is explored. In this section, the HDG will be used to test Moffitt's hypotheses about the manifestations of antisocial behavior in the Life-Course-Persistent offending group, as it most closely approximates her LCP group.

Suspension data was collected by the Baltimore City Public Schools for fourth through seventh grades. When examining the percentage of individuals who were suspended one or more times during each school year, there does appear to be a difference across the three groups. The Abstainers (AB) had a very low suspension rate where the LCPs and the ALs have much higher rates. In fact, in sixth grade, the LCP group had a suspension rate five times higher than the AB group. It is interesting that the LCP and AL groups appear to have very similar suspension rates, but it is clear that they are distinctly different than the AB group.

Figure 20. School Suspensions by Posterior Class Probability

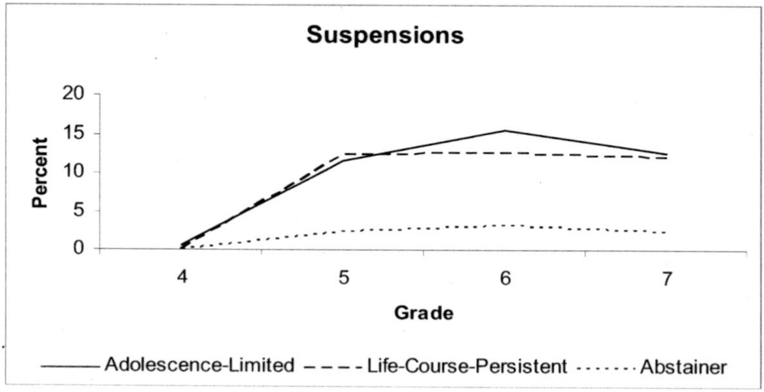

The subjects were asked "have you ever used tobacco" each year from sixth through twelfth grades in an interview. The groups are distinctly different in how quickly they initiate smoking behavior. As anticipated by Moffitt, fewer of the AB group engaged in smoking behavior and they appeared to have a later onset. Also predicted by the taxonomy, the AL group experienced the highest rates of tobacco incidence.

Over half of the sample had used alcohol by sixth grade, the first year the question was asked, which is interesting since delinquency appears to be such a low base-rate behavior in the classroom. The groups were not different in sixth grade or at any other time period. It appears that drinking is a behavior with a younger initiation age, and that each of the groups experiences the same pattern in initiation into drinking behavior. Of course, this only measures the age of onset, not frequency or severity of the alcohol use, which could still differ by group.

Figure 21. **Tobacco Use Initiation by Posterior Class Probability**

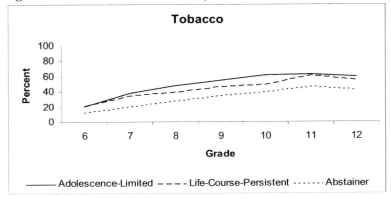

Figure 22. **Alcohol Initiation by Posterior Class Probability**

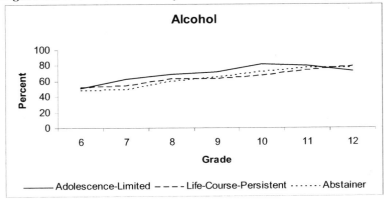

In sixth grade, very few subjects reported having tried marijuana (AB=2.3%, AL=6.3%, LCP=5.7%). The AL group used marijuana at an earlier age, and continued to be initiated at a quicker rate. By twelfth grade, over 60% of the AL group reported having tried marijuana, whereas only 40% of the AB group has experimented with marijuana. The LCP group remained in between the AB and LCP groups, with half of them reporting that they had tried the drug by the twelfth grade.

Figure 23. *Marijuana Use by Posterior Class Probability*

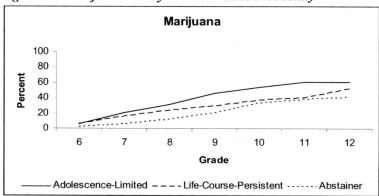

At the first collection period, sixth grade, about eight percent of the subjects reported having used illicit drugs (AL=9.8%, LCP=7.5%, AB=7.8%). These numbers are higher than the marijuana figures, and therefore it can be deduced that while many of the subjects may be reporting marijuana use, there are still some that are experimenting with other illicit drugs. By the end of the data collection period, however, the numbers are identical to the marijuana figures. The group patterns are exactly the same as the previous figure tracking marijuana initiation; with the AL group becoming involved in illicit drug use the most frequently and quickly, the AB group having fewer members experimenting with illicit drugs, and the LCP group falling in between the other two groups.

In sixth grade, 57% and 55% of the AL and LCP group members reported having used a drug while only 49% of the AB group experimented with any drugs. The AL group reported the highest rates of trying drugs throughout middle and high school, although the group differences were decreasing by the end of high school. By twelfth grade, over 80% of the AL group reported experimenting with any drug, as opposed to the 60% who admitting trying illicit drugs. The same pattern held true for the LCP group, with over 80% reporting trying a drug by twelfth grade but only 51% divulging that they had engaged in illicit drug use. Interestingly, almost 80% of the AB confessed to trying a drug by twelfth grade, but only 42% claimed to have tried an illicit drug. These are very high rates for a group that is "abstaining" from delinquent behavior. It appears that they may be experimenting with drug use at the same rate as their counterparts, but instead using socially and legally acceptable drugs.

Figure 24. Illicit Drug Initiation by Posterior Class Probability

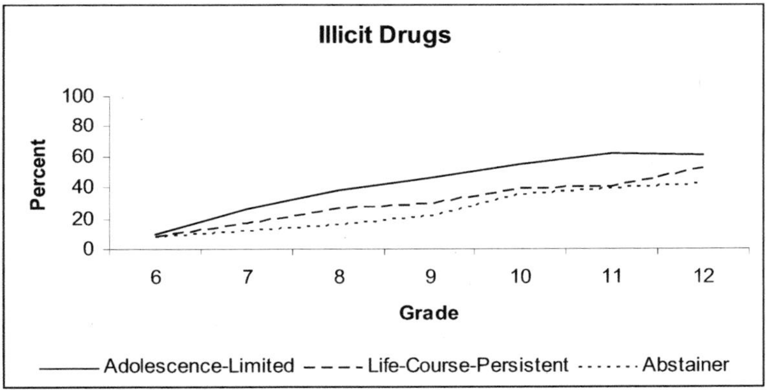

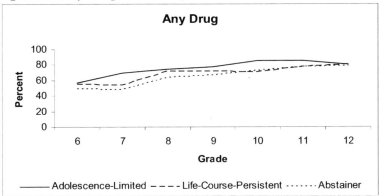

Figure 25. Any Drug Initiation by Posterior Class Probability

Overall, the pattern of school suspensions and substance use initiation is compatible with Moffitt's theory. The LCP and AL groups has a higher suspension rate than the AB group. According to Moffitt, the disparity between the AL and AB group in terms of antisocial behavior should not appear until puberty. The difference in suspension rates appear in the fifth grade, which would be expected, as females experience puberty between 8 and 13 years of age, and male from 9.5 to 14 years of age.

Also in accordance with Moffitt's predictions, the AB group members report abstaining from all substance use for the longest (although 80% have experimented with "any drug" by twelfth grade) and the AL group has a younger average age of onset and has more group members experimenting with cigarettes, alcohol, marijuana, and illicit drugs. Since these measures do not reflect either frequency or severity of substance use, the only conclusions that can be drawn are that there does appear to be a relationship between group membership and age of onset for tobacco, marijuana, and illicit drug use.

While the data generally support Moffitt's theory, they are far from a perfect fit. A much higher percentage of the abstainers are experimenting with substances, such as tobacco, alcohol, marijuana, and illicit drugs, than would be expected. The adolescence-limited group does have a lower initiation age into experimentation with illegal substances and a greater percentage of group members reporting experimentation, but it is not always significantly different (e.g., alcohol use).

SUMMARY

This chapter focused on selecting which of the models from the previous chapter best fit Moffitt's theory and the data. Each of the different combinations of freed and fixed variances in the latent growth terms has different implications for the meaning of a "group" and the heterogeneity of the individuals that make up that group. Despite the different restrictions placed in the models, the results were very similar for those that allowed different variances to be estimated in at least one of the latent growth terms.

It appears that loosening the restrictions on the variance invariance between classes significantly changes the make-up of the groups without appreciably impacting the latent growth parameters. A more elaborate set of parameters are needed to identify the models that include variance, and this brings up essential theoretical issues about the meaning of groups when they are made up of heterogeneous subpopulations. Despite the drawbacks of estimating variances and covariances separately for each group, the most complex approach, which estimated variances in both the latent growth parameters separately, was selected as superior because of the fit statistics, theoretical meaning, and class proportions. The limitations to selecting this model are in its complexity and the meaningfulness of group membership. The model with the least restrictive variance structure necessitates estimating more parameters than any of the other models, which created a less parsimonious model.

The final model selected was a three group model. This study did find a group that displayed a higher level of delinquency in the classroom which could resemble Moffitt's life-course-persistent group; however, the group did not remain higher than the others over time. The group, which could be characterized as high declining group (HDG), had an intercept was three times higher than the other groups, but it also had a negative slope. A second group approximated Moffitt's AL group, but it did not exactly match her hypotheses. The group does increase through adolescence, though not as dramatically as would be expected. Additionally, it appears that the delinquency ratings peak in the beginning of adolescence (sixth grade, Mean=2.5) and appear to decrease before the end of adolescence. Finally, the last group matched Moffitt's abstainer group, although, its trajectory was not exactly as Moffitt predicted. This group always displayed the lowest delinquency ratings, but there delinquency scores were always significantly higher than zero.[12] They also did experience a very small increase in delinquency scores over time. The shape of the AB group's trajectory is the closest to Moffitt's predictions.

With the fundamental issue of the validity and reliability of trajectory group membership in dispute, the external validity of group membership is exceedingly important. Differences between trajectory group members on alternative measures of delinquency, such as suspension rates, alcohol, tobacco, marijuana, and other drug use initiation, were used to test whether group membership is meaningful across theoretically-relevant factors. In line with Moffitt's predictions, the AB group members report abstaining from all substance use for the

---

[12] Several different methods for fixing the abstaining group to have zero delinquency were attempted over the course of the study; however these models did not converge. It did not appear that there was truly a "zero delinquency" or abstaining group.

longest and the AL group has a younger average age of onset and a larger percent of its group members experimenting with cigarettes, alcohol, marijuana, and illicit drugs. It is important to note that these measures do not represent either frequency or severity of substance use.

These findings provide some support Moffitt's theory; though they are far from conclusive evidence of the external validity of group membership. For instance, contrary to Moffitt's hypotheses, a much higher percentage of the abstainers are experimenting with substances, such as tobacco, alcohol, marijuana, and illicit drugs, than would be expected. Of course, there are many more AB group members than she would have predicted, and perhaps there are actually more distinct groups that were not uncovered empirically using the aggression/disruption scale which are diluting the sample and influencing the results. Also, while the adolescence-limited group does have a lower initiation age into experimentation with illegal substances and a greater percentage of group members reporting experimentation, it is not always significantly different than the other groups (e.g., alcohol use).

This chapter established that group-based trajectory modeling was able to capture the development of delinquency in the classroom better than a single group model (traditional growth curve modeling). The three group model with variance in the intercept and slope factors that varies both between and within group was found to best fit the data theoretically and empirically. The group trajectories provided partial support for Moffitt's theory: there were three groups, as anticipated; however, the shape of the growth curves and class proportions were not aligned with her predictions.

A group that displayed a higher level of delinquency in the classroom was uncovered, but they also declined with age, which was not anticipated by Moffitt. A second group increased through adolescence, but did not experience as a dramatic of an increase was anticipated. The third group matched Moffitt's abstainer group which always displayed the lowest delinquency ratings. According to her theory, the majority of the sample should have followed the AL pattern, not the AB pattern, and the highest group should not have exhibited a negative slope. However, the group members did differ in alternate measures of delinquency in the way that her theory anticipated, including differential suspension rates, and onset of tobacco, alcohol, and drug use. Therefore, in the remainder of this research, the High

Declining Group (HDG) will be referred to as the Life-Course-Persistent Group (LCP) to remain consistent and compare them with Moffitt's Taxonomy.

CHAPTER 8.

Moffitt's Predictors of Group Membership

This chapter explores Moffitt's predictors of delinquency trajectories and group membership. Moffitt's taxonomy includes hypotheses about the characteristics of the life-course-persistent, adolescence-limited, and abstainer groups. Variables collected from parent, teacher, and student interviews were used to represent constructs such as individual psycho-physiological dysfunction, environmental dysfunction, deviant peer affiliation, and positive peer bonding, each of which should predict group membership. When adding covariates to predict group membership, the trajectories can shift, both in intercept and slope and in class proportion. Therefore, class membership must be reevaluated once the predictors have been added.

This chapter concentrates on the set of research questions concerning Moffitt's hypothesized predictors of the different types of delinquents. The LCP group should show evidence of early behavioral problems in childhood across multiple domains, early psycho-physiological problems, and environmental and/or contextual dysfunction. The AL group should parallel the AB group in childhood, and only differ from them in their experiences with the maturity gap and access to deviant peer role models. Finally, the AB group may show evidence of some resilience factor that is preventing the members from engaging in antisocial or delinquent behavior.

Each of the sets of hypothesized predictors that should be related to offender type was entered into separate models to determine which of the variables are empirically related to trajectory group membership. These predictors were added into a single-growth model in order to determine if group-based trajectory modeling is still necessary once predictors were added. The single group and three group models were tested against each other.

107

Figure 26. Covariates Predicting a Single Group Model

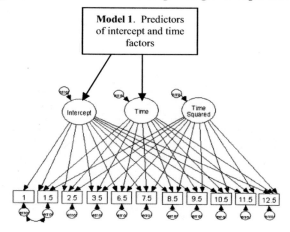

Figure 27. Adding Covariates to a General Growth Mixture Model

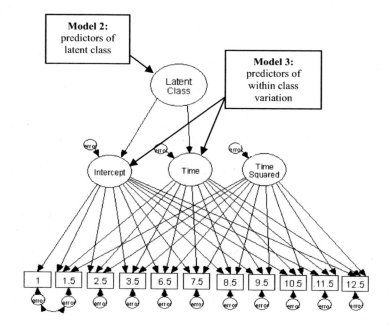

If it is determined that modeling trajectory groups significantly increases model fit, the significant predictors were explored and differences in group membership were investigated. The covariates were entered as (A) predictors of class membership and (B) interindividual variability within classes in separate models. Predicting within group variation represents the covariates as mediator variables and not predictors of class membership. The two ways of adding the covariates are be explored and tested against one another in this chapter.

ABSTAINER COVARIATES

According to Moffitt, abstainers do not feel the same motivation to engage in delinquent behavior because of their lack of experience with the maturity gap. Since there were no measures of physical or social maturity in this dataset, it is impossible to test this hypothesis. However, there was a measurement of social bonding, which has been demonstrated to be a protective factor in previous research (Hawkins, Catalano, & Miller, 1992).

Abstainer Model Specifics

The friendship scale was added into the model in three ways: (1) as a covariate for a single group model, (2) as a predictor of class in a group-based model, and (3) as a predictor of within class variation in a group-based model. Adding the friendship scale significantly improved model fit over the baseline three group model that was established in the previous chapters. The models that included groups were both significantly a better fit than the single class model.[13] The entropy increased from .78 to .81, but the rest of the model remained essentially unchanged.

None of the parameters changed significantly from the baseline model, and therefore are not reported here. Although the fit statistics appear marginally better with the covariate predicting the within class variation model than the model predicting class membership, it also estimates far more parameters, and is a far less parsimonious model. Therefore, the model predicting class was selected as a better fit.

---

[13] Likelihood ratio: $\chi^2(10)=577.72$, p<.001 and $\chi^2(10)=572.84$, respectfully.

Table 26. *Abstainer Model*

	AIC	BIC	SSA BIC	Ent.	LL	Class Proportions
Baseline Model	11083.7	10283.9	10788.7	.78	-5044.19	LCP: 11% AL: 24% AB: 65%
Model 1: Covariates on 1 Group	10007.4	10094.3	10030.8	NA	-4983.70	
Model 2: Covariates on Class	9575.54	9705.91	9610.68	.81	-4757.77	LCP: 11% AL: 25% AB: 65%
Model 3: Covariates on w/i class var	9570.67	9701.93	9605.80	.81	-4755.33	LCP: 11% AL: 23% AB: 66%

The friendship scale is a significant predictor of trajectory class membership. Individuals with higher scores on the friendship importance scale were more likely to belong to the AB group than the AL. There was no difference between scores on the friendship scale and the AB verses the LCP group while the theory would predict that friendship importance, or social bonding, should be higher in the AB group than the LCP group.

Table 27. *Abstainer Model Predictors*

	Parameterization using ABSTAINERS as Reference	
	Adolescence-Limited	Life-Course-Persistent
Friendship Importance	-.62**	-.03

The more importance placed on close friendship, the more likely the subject is to belong to the AB class and the less important a subject claims close friendship is, the more likely the individual is to belong to the AL group. Friendship importance is not helpful in predicting LCP group membership, which is contrary to Moffitt's theory, which states that LCP offenders are likely to reject friendships. It offers partial support for social bonding, in that it appears to be a resilience factor to delinquency.

Figure 28. Friendship on Probability of Group Membership

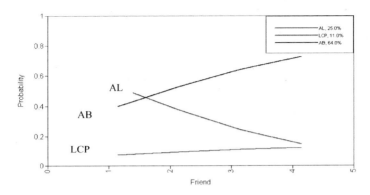

Friend

Abstainer Model Group Members

Individuals' group membership did not change a great deal from the baseline model when the abstainer predictor was added. The pseudo class membership is virtually identical to the one from the baseline model, with only 14 individuals switching "most likely" class. The new AL group absorbed ten individuals from both the AB and LCP groups, the LCP groups are identical, and four individuals changed into the AB group from the LCP the AL groups. The overall 2% change in group membership did not change the group profiles in respect to member demographics by posterior group membership probability.

Table 28. Group Member Assignments: Baseline and Abstainer Models

	Abstainer Covariate Model Assignment		
Baseline Assignment	AL Group	LCP Group	AB Group
AL Group	99.2%, N=120	0%, N=0	.8%, N=1
LCP Group	4.5%, N=3	91.0%, N=61	4.5%, N=3
AB Group	1.8%, N=7	0%, N=0%	98.2%, N=374

ADOLESCENCE-LIMITED PREDICTORS

According to Moffitt, adolescence-limited offending is caused by the maturity gap, a disconnect between physical and social maturity. In order to fully test this hypothesis, measures of physical and social maturity are necessary; however, this data is not available for this dataset. She predicts that due to the maturity gap, adolescents act out and mimic antisocial behavior in order to achieve some level of social maturity. The availability of delinquent peer role models plays an important part of the learning and mimicry process. Measures of delinquent peers and neighborhood were used to test this portion of her theory – while adolescence-limited offenders did not necessarily have to befriend delinquent peers, they must at the very least observe them, which is why both delinquent peers and neighborhood constructs are essential parts of this model.

Adolescence-Limited Model Specifics

The adolescence-limited covariates were added into the model in three ways: (1) as covariates for a single group model, (2) as predictors of class in a group-based model, and (3) as predictors of within class variation in a group-based model. Entering the two adolescence-limited predictors increases the model fit from the baseline three group model, regardless of how they were entered. Both models that include trajectory group fit the data better than the single group model, and better than the three class model without predictors.[14] Adding the covariates as predictors of class membership fits the data better than predicting within group variation, and therefore, it is selected as the superior model. The model predicting class membership does not significantly affect the class proportions or any of the model parameters from the baseline model. The growth curves look virtually identical to those in the three class unequal variance model described in the earlier chapters.

Both of the predictors of AL group membership were significant in this model. Those who scored higher on the deviant peers were more likely to belong to the AL group, as anticipated by Moffitt's theory. High scorers were also more likely to belong to the LCP group than the AB group, but there was no significant difference in scores on the deviant peer measurement and belonging to the AL verses the LCP group. The neighborhood variable significantly predicted membership in the AL group from both the AB and LCP groups, as predicted by Moffitt's taxonomy.

---

[14] Likelihood ratio: $\chi^2(12)=588.92$, p<.001 and $\chi^2(12)=511.86$, respectfully

Table 29. Adolescence-Limited Model

	AIC	BIC	SSA BIC	Entropy	LL	Class Proportions
Baseline Model	11083.71	10283.90	10788.65	.78	-5044.2	LCP: 11% AL: 24% AB: 65%
Model 1. Covariate on 1 Class	1007.40	10094.31	10030.82	NA	-4983.7	
Model 2. Covariates on Class	9564.47	9702.53	9600.94	.82	-4749.7	LCP: 11% AL: 24% AB: 65%
Model 3. Covariates on w/i Class Var.	9641.93	9780.99	9679.41	.67	-4789.0	LCP: 6.3% AL: 33% AB: 61%

Table 30. Adolescence-Limited Model Predictors

	Parameterization using ADOLESCENCE-LIMITED as Reference	
	Abstainer	Life-Course-Persistent
Deviant Peers	-.64**	.20
Neighborhood	-.96**	-1.02**

Examining the probability plots of group membership by the covariate, it is clear that the probability of belonging to the AB group if an individual scores low on either the deviant peers or the neighborhood scale is high, and decreases as scores go up. The probability of belonging to the AL and LCP groups increase with higher scores on the deviant peers scale. The probability of being a AL group member increases as the neighborhood score increases, and decreases the probability of being a LCP or AB offender type.

Figure 29. *Deviant Peers on the Probability of Group Membership*

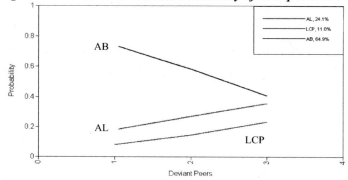

Figure 30. *Neighborhood on the Probability of Group Membership*

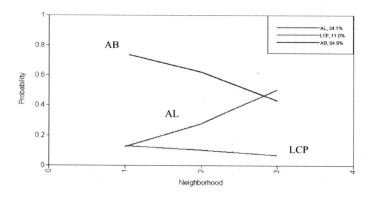

Adolescence-Limited Model Group Members

As the model did not change a great deal, most of the individuals did not change groups based on the addition of the deviant peers and neighborhood predictors. A total of 21 people (less than 4% of the sample) changed most likely trajectory class. The new AB group picked up ten individuals total, the LCP group gained one member, and the AL group added ten members. The overall 4% change in group membership did not change the group profiles in respect to member demographics by posterior class probability.

Table 31. Group Member Assignments: Baseline and Adolescence-Limited Models

Baseline Assignment	Adolescence-Limited Covariate Model Assignment		
	AL Group	LCP Group	AB Group
AL Group	95.0%, N=120	.8%, N=1	4.5%, N=5
LCP Group	3.0%, N=2	89.6%, N=60	7.5%, N=5
AB Group	2.1%, N=8	0%, N=0%	97.9%, N=373

Life-Course-Persistent Predictors

According to Moffitt, a confluence of psycho-physiological and environmental dysfunction should be found in the background of the life-course-persistent offenders. In this section, four variables that represent psycho-physiological dysfunction and two that represent environmental problems were selected.

The first four predictors represent psychological difficulties: (1) concentration problems, (2) hyperactivity, (3) anxiety, and (4) depression. The first two were found to be associated with delinquency scores, while the other two were not. The final two predictors captured parenting practices, such as inconsistent disciplinary practices and monitoring. Overall, neither of the two parenting constructs was found to be correlated with delinquency scores at any one time, with the exception of the small relationship between monitoring and delinquency at a few of the time periods.

Life-Course-Persistent Model Specifics

The LCP predictors were added into the model in three ways: (1) as covariates for a single group model, (2) as predictors of class in a group-based model, and (3) as predictors of within class variation in a group-based model. The hyperactivity score appeared to display a curvilinear relationship with probability of group membership within the adolescence-limited group, and therefore a squared hyperactivity term was added to the class-specific adolescence-limited model, but not the others.

Figure 31. *Curvilinear Relationship of Hyperactivity within AL Class*

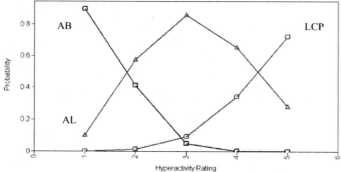

Both models that included trajectory group performed significantly better than the one that only modeled one group.[15] After adding the predictors, the class proportions in both models also changed, with the AB group diminishing from 65% of the sample to 48%, and the AL group gaining 18% of the sample in the class prediction model. The entropy also increased in this model, meaning that with the addition of the six predictors, the classification ability of the model was improved. The class prediction model (Model 2) was selected as superior because the entropy is higher (from .78 to .86) and the class proportions are improved. It was selected above the model in which the covariates predicted within class variation because the information criterions are so similar but the model is much more parsimonious and consistent with Moffitt's theory.

In addition to changing the class proportions from the baseline model, adding the covariates changed the intercepts and slopes of each trajectory class. The LCP group's initial delinquency ratings went from 3.67 to 3.88, and the slope factor decreased from -.32 to -.28. The AL group's intercept increased from 1.36 to 1.68, and the slope decreased by half, from .30 to .14. The AB group became much more homogeneous, with an initial delinquency rating of 1.13 (down from 1.32) with no variation, and a very small slope (.06). Only two of the predictors were significantly related to trajectory class, concentration and hyperactivity.

---

[15] Likelihood ratio: $\chi^2(10)=1223.40$, p<.001 and $\chi^2(8)=1263.78$, p<.001, respectfully

Table 32. Life-Course-Persistent Model

	AIC	BIC	SSA BIC	Entropy	LL	Class Proportions
<u>Baseline</u> <u>Model</u>	11083.71	10283.90	10788.65	.78	-5044.2	LCP: 11% AL: 24% AB: 65%
Model 1. Covariate on 1 Class	9207.57	9338.92	9243.67	NA	-4573.8	
Model 2. Covariates on Class	8944.97	9120.97	8993.12	.86	-4432.5	LCP: 10% AL: 42% AB: 48%
Model 3. Covariates on w/i Class Var	8908.61	9092.50	8959.17	.85	-4412.3	LCP: 7% AL: 11% AB: 82%

Figure 32. Growth Trajectories by Class with Life-Course-Persistent Predictors

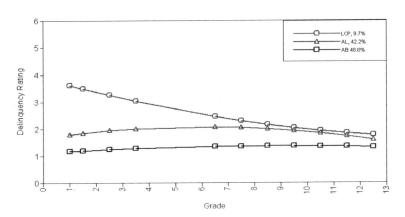

Table 33. *Life-Course-Persistent Model Predictors*

	Parameterization using LIFE-COURSE-PERSISTENTS as Reference	
	Adolescence-Limited	Abstainers
Concentration	-.89**	-1.61**
Hyperactivity	-6.14**	-6.14**
Hyperactivity^2	.71**	*NA*
Anxiety	1.13	1.83
Depression	.25	-.29
Parent Discipline	.56	.34
Parent Monitoring	.33	.58

Examining the probability plots of group membership by the covariate, it is clear that the probability of belonging to the AB group is high for individuals who score low on either the concentration or the hyperactivity scale, and it decreases as scores go up. The probability of belonging to the AL group increases with higher scores on the concentration scale, but interestingly, the relationship between hyperactivity and group membership is curvilinear. The probability of belonging to the AL group peaks in the middle of the hyperactivity score range, and decreases both above and below. The probability of belonging to the LCP group is always lower because it has a low base rate, but it is highest at the high ends of the concentration and hyperactivity scales.

Figure 33. *Concentration on the Probability of Group Membership*

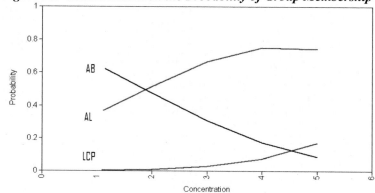

Figure 34. Hyperactivity on the Probability of Group Membership

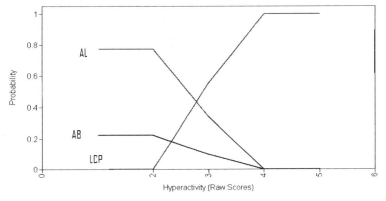

Hyperactivity (Raw Scores)

Life-Course-Persistent Model Group Members

Adding the predictors in the LCP model changed the group membership significantly. Over one-quarter of the subjects were reassigned to a different trajectory group. The most frequent shift was from the baseline model's AB group to the new model's AL group (n=128, or 22% of the entire sample). This shift in group membership caused the AL trajectory group means to be lowered and the AL and LCP trajectories no longer cross.

Table 34. Group Member Assignments: Baseline and Life-Course-Persistent Models

Baseline Assignment	LCP Covariate Model Assignment		
	AL Group	LCP Group	AB Group
AL Group	91.2%, N=104	.9%, N=1	7.9%, N=9
LCP Group	16.4%, N=11	83.6%, N=56	0%, N=0
AB Group	31.4%, N=128	0%, N=0	68.6%, N=279

Although there was a redistribution of 25% of population to different trajectory classes, only one variable in the demographic profiles of the groups changed significantly. After adding the LCP covariates, the gender distribution within the AL class changed, with significantly fewer males and more females in the AL group. The rest of the differences were within the 95% confidence interval.

Table 35. Comparison of Group Members from Baseline to Life-Course-Persistent Covariate Model

	Adolescence-Limited		Life-Course-Persistent		Adolescence-Limited	
	Baseline Model N=164	Covariate Model N=136	Baseline Model N=75	Covariate Model N=76	Baseline Model N=438	Covariate Model N=465
Sex						
Male	*68.4%**	*62.0%**	77.7%	79.0%	43.5%	39.6%
Femal	*31.6%**	*38.0%**	22.3%	21.0%	56.5%	60.4%
Race						
White	12.4%	11.7%	18.6%	18.1%	13.0%	15.3%
Black.	87.4%	88.3%	81.4%	81.9%	87.0%	84.7%
Cond						
No	38.1%	29.4%	26.9%	21.6%	31.1%	33.7%
CC	30.0%	33.4%	43.3%	42.2%	33.9%	33.5%
FSP	31.9%	37.2%	29.8%	36.2%	35.0%	32.8%
Age	6.22	6.24	6.26	6.30	6.22	6.21
Incom						
<$5K	16.4%	15.9%	21.2%	22.4%	10.2%	6.6%
$5K	18.5%	18.7%	17.5%	20.8%	16.0%	15.2%
$10K	23.1%	21.8%	*20.7%*	18.5%	21.8%	23.6%
$20K	18.8%	20.1%	17.1%	16.0%	20.8%	21.2%
$30K	18.4%	16.8%	14.9%	16.1%	24.4%	27.9%
Fam						
2 Par	42.7%	47.0%	36.1%	35.5%	53.4%	55.7%
1 Par	49.0%	45.3%	54.0%	52.7%	40.3%	38.9%

* p<.05

SUMMARY

This chapter explored Moffitt's predictors of delinquency trajectories and group membership.   The following set of research questions concerning Moffitt's hypothesized predictors of the different types of delinquents:

1. The LCP group should show evidence of early behavioral problems in childhood across multiple domains, early psycho-physiological problems, and environmental and/or contextual dysfunction.

2. The AL group should parallel the AB group in childhood, and only differ from them in their experiences with the maturity gap and access to deviant peer role models.

3. Finally, the AB group may show evidence of some resilience factor that is preventing the members from engaging in antisocial or delinquent behavior.

Her hypotheses about the characteristics of the life-course-persistent, adolescence-limited, and abstainer groups were entered into separate models to determine whether they do in fact predict group membership. The predictors were also added in two other ways in order to determine empirically how they influence delinquency: (1) as predictors of a general growth model to test whether the predictors are simply explaining the variance in the intercept and slope factors, which would mean group-based trajectory modeling is only capturing artificial cutoffs in the normal distribution, (2) as predictors of group membership, and (3) as predictors of within class variability. In each case, the model fit increased the most when adding the covariates as predictors of class, as is anticipated by the theory.

The results provided partial support for Moffitt's hypotheses. The AB model found that friendship importance is a significant predictor of abstaining from delinquency, and could differentiate between abstainers and adolescence-limited offenders. Adding this covariate did not significantly change group membership. The AL model found that both exposure to deviant peers and living in a neighborhood that is perceived to be more criminogenic significantly predict group membership in the direction that Moffitt suggested. Adding the AL covariates did not drastically alter group membership either. There were many more covariates added to the LCP model, but only two were significantly associated with group membership. The mental health indicators (depression and anxiety), and parenting measurements were not significant predictors of LCP group membership. Children displaying higher levels of concentration problems and hyperactivity, however, were more likely to belong to the LCP and AL groups than the AB group. Once these predictors were added to the model, over one-quarter of the sample changed most likely trajectory group.

Overall, the results provide partial support for Moffitt's hypotheses. The AB and AL models found relationships that were anticipated by her theory. Deviant peers and neighborhoods differentiated abstainers from adolescence-limited offenders, but deviant peers also distinguished abstainers from life-course-persistent offenders, which was not specifically projected by Moffitt's theory. The largest discrepancy between the theory and the findings from these analyses was in the LCP model. Several of the variables that Moffitt predicted would be associated with life-course-persistent offending were found to be insignificant (depression, anxiety, parental monitoring, parental discipline). Even more troubling in respect to her taxonomy, was the relationship between concentration problems and adolescence-limiting offending. According to her theory, there should be no differences between AB and AL group members on these variables, but this study did find a significant difference. It appears that concentration problems and hyperactivity distinguish AB group members from both AL and LCP.

CHAPTER 9.

Comprehensively Testing Moffitt's Theory

This chapter combines the models run in the previous chapter that represent each of the sets of predictors for trajectory groups into one model. Several models are examined and their similarities and differences scrutinized. Building on the previous chapters, this section proposes a final group-based model with predictors and demographic controls to test Moffitt's developmental taxonomy. After the model is established, the group members and concurrent validity of group membership are reconsidered.

EXPLORING MODELS

The final model includes all of the predictors that were significant in the previous chapter[16]: (1) concentration, (2) hyperactivity, (3) peer deviance, (4) neighborhood deviance, and (5) friends.[17] After this

---

[16] When adding the five predictors, the model selected in the previous chapter is unidentified because it required the estimation of too many the latent variances and covariances. In order for the model to converge, variance restrictions had to be placed on the model. The variance in the intercept factor was fixed to be equal across groups for purposes of model convergence. This restriction was selected because when they were estimated separately, they were statistically equivalent, so fixing them to be equal simply increased the degrees of freedom without significantly altering the parameterization. Once this restriction was placed, the model could be estimated.

[17] The squared hyperactivity term was removed from the AL submodel because it caused serious model convergence problems due to the smaller sample size and loss of power. The estimated parameters from the models including the squared hyperactivity term were essentially unchanged, and therefore it does not appear that removing the term significantly altered the model parameters or fit statistics.

model is estimated, race and gender will be added to see how and if they impact the model.

Covariate Model without Demographic Controls

Each of the five covariates is significantly associated with group membership except the neighborhood deviance construct. The intercepts and slopes, along with the class proportions, were also notably different than the baseline model. Adding the five predictors on class membership resulted in a better fit than the one class model with the same predictors.[18]

Figure 35. Group Trajectories without Demographic Controls

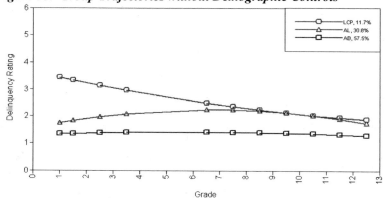

Almost all of the relationships are aligned with Moffitt's predictions: (1) poor concentration and hyperactivity predict LCP group membership, (2) peer deviance predicts AL group membership, and (3) friendship importance predicts AB group membership. Peer deviance also predicts LCP group membership, which is not explicitly anticipated by her theory, as she believes that LCP offenders are rejected by their peers and may be loners; however, the fact that they appear to have more delinquent peers does fit with other aspects of her theory. The only relationship in direct opposition with her taxonomy is the relationship between poor concentration and hyperactivity and AL

---

[18] $\chi^2(5)$=2099.50, p<.001

group membership – according to Moffitt's theory, there should be no difference in concentration levels in childhood between members of the AL and AB groups.

Table 36. Final Model Predictors without Demographic Controls

	Parameterization using ABSTAINERS as Reference		Parameterization using LIFE-COURSE-PERSISTENTS as Reference
	AL	LCP	AL
Concentration	.77**	1.51**	-.73**
Hyperactivity	1.53	3.39**	-1.87**
Peer Deviance	1.02**	1.96**	-.95**
Neighborhood	.53	.09	.44
Friendship	-.048**	.37	-.85**

Covariate Model with Demographic Controls

The demographic controls of gender and race can be added in two ways, either as predictors of group membership or as predictors of within group variation. They were added both ways, and the model predicting class membership from the demographics performed better and will be the only model reported in this section. The neighborhood deviance construct was also eliminated from the model because it was found to be not significant in the previous model.

Both the demographic control variables were significant predictors of group membership, with females being less likely to be in either the AL or LCP group compared to the AB group. [19] African-American

---

[19] As there were more predictors, more restrictions were necessary for model identification. The previous model fixed the within group intercept variation to be equal across classes (variance invariance), and even further restrictions were necessary for the model with demographic controls because of the addition of more predictors. On top of the variance invariance restriction placed on the intercept factor, the slope variance had to be fixed to zero because it was so highly (and negatively) correlated with the intercept variance that it produced a negative variance when it was estimated. This negative variation was not statistically different from zero, so restricting it to equal zero did not significantly impact the parameterization of the model. Once these restrictions were placed on the model, it was able to converge.

students were more likely to belong to the AB group than the AL or LCP groups as well.

The majority of the relationships support Moffitt's theory. LCP group members are more likely to display poor concentration and hyperactivity in childhood, AL group members are more likely to have deviant peers in adolescence, and AB group members are more likely to believe friendship is important in adolescence (strong social bonds). Unanticipated findings include hyperactivity activity levels distinguishing AB from AL group members, and LCP group members experiencing higher levels of deviant peer affiliation in adolescence than AB group members.

Table 37. Final Models with Demographic Controls

	Parameterization using ABSTAINERS as Reference		Parameterization using LCP as Reference
	AL	LCP	AL
Female	-1.73**	-2.19**	.45
African-American	-.70**	-1.67**	.97*
Concentration	.36	.95**	-.60**
Hyperactivity	1.49**	2.76**	-1.27
Peer Deviance	1.45**	1.41**	.04
Friendship	-.62**	.01	-.63

Adding the demographic controls also significantly impact the class proportions and the shapes of the trajectories, although some of this could be due to the tightened variance restrictions that had to be placed in order for the model to converge. Eleven percent of the population changed classes when adding this group of predictors, and the intercept and slope were also impacted, see the group trajectories with demographic controls below. The majority of the class changes were individuals who were classified as AL moving to the AB group.

Figure 36. Group Trajectories with Demographic Controls

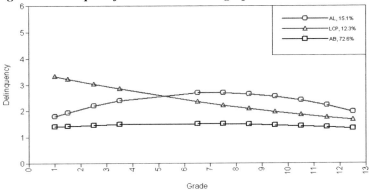

COMPARING MODELS

Each of the covariate models produced better fit statistics than the baseline model, and each of the covariate models that included latent trajectory class was a better fit than the predictors influencing the latent intercept and slope factors in a one class model. The models are also strikingly similar, with almost all the parameters being essentially equal. Comparing the baseline model with the final models that included the combination of predictors from the AB-, AL-, and LCP-specific models, the intercept means were almost all within the 95% confidence interval (AL: 1.16 – 1.56, LCP: 3.25 – 4.08, and AB: 1.22 – 1.42). The only model that was not equivalent was the LCP-specific model, which had a lower intercept for the AB group and a higher one for the AL group. The same pattern held for the slopes; they were all within a 95% confidence interval as well, (AL: .20 – .40, LCP: -.22 to -.42, and AB: .03 - .05), with the exception of the AB and AL groups in the LCP-specific model.

The other fit statistics are difficult to compare across models because they are dealing with a slightly different set of the data. Each model includes a slightly different make-up of the sample because subjects must have complete data on all of the predictors in order to be included in any model. Due to this fact, the more predictors that were included in any particular model, the fewer subjects were used in the model and each had a slightly different sample.

Table 38. Final Models with Demographic Controls

	Baseline Model	LCP Model	AL Model	AB Model	Combined Model	Combined Model with Dems
Entropy	.78	.86	.82	.81	.83	.89
AIC	10294.04	8944.97	9563.47	9575.54	9163.05	9306.78
BIC	10420.58	9120.11	9702.53	9705.91	9322.79	9462.20
SSA BIC	10331.67	8993.12	9600.94	9610.68	9205.33	9347.92
-2 LL	-5119.20	-4432.49	-4749.73	-4757.77	-4544.53	-4617.39
Adolescence-Limited						
Intercept μ	1.36 (.10)	1.68 (.09)	1.39 (.10)	1.41 (.11)	1.55 (.26)	1.48 (.23)
Intercept σ	.19 (.03)	.07 (.05)	.19 (.03)	.19 (.03)	*Fixed to* .05 (.10)	*Fixed to* .07 (.01)
Slope μ	.30 (.05)	.14 (.03)	.30 (.05)	.29 (.05)	.21 (.12)	.35 (.08)
Slope σ	*Fixed to 0*	.002 (.001)	.002 (.001)	.002 (.00)	.003 (.001)	*Fixed to 0*
Proportion	24.4%	42%	24%	25%	31%	15%
Life-Course-Persistent						
Intercept μ	3.67 (.21)	3.88 (.17)	3.80 (.20)	3.80 (.20)	3.65 (.18)	3.54 (.22)
Intercept σ	.19 (.03)	.06 (.05)	.19 (.03)	.19 (.03)	*Fixed to* .05 (.10)	*Fixed to* .07 (.01)
Slope μ	-.32 (.05)	-.27 (.07)	-.32 (.05)	-.32 (.05)	-.22 (.06)	-.22 (.06)
Slope σ	.002 (.00)	.002 (.001)	.002 (.001)	.002 (.001)	.003 (.001)	*Fixed to 0*
Proportion	11.1%	10%	11%	11%	12%	12%
"abstainer"						
Intercept μ	1.32 (.05)	1.13 (.03)	1.34 (.05)	1.34 (.05)	1.68 (.09)	1.37 (.03)
Intercept σ	.08 (.03)	.00 (.01)	.10 (.03)	.10 (.03)	.06 (.05)	*Fixed to* .07 (.01)
Slope μ	.04 (.009)	.05 (.01)	.04 (.01)	.04 (.01)	.14 (.03)	.05 (.01)
Slope σ	.000 (.00)	.00 (.00)	.001 (.00)	.001 (.00)	.002 (.001)	*Fixed to 0*
Proportion	64.5%	48%	65%	64%	57%	73%

However, there are some interesting patterns that can be considered: (1) the entropy increased when adding predictors, with the highest entropy in the model with all the covariates plus the demographic controls., (2) the proportion of individuals in the LCP group remained exceedingly stable (between 10% and 12%)[20], and (3) adding predictors to class membership always outperforms adding them as predictors of within class variation.

The major differences between the models are in the variance assumptions around the latent intercept and slope factors. The baseline model and AB-, AL-, and LCP-specific models assume unequal variance between groups in the latent growth factors. While this assumption was explored in previous analyses and deemed to be the most appropriate assumption to fit both the data and the theory, it was statistically unworkable when adding a large number of covariates to the model. It was necessary to fix some of the latent variances to be equal across groups for the first full model and some to be zero for the full model that included demographic controls. It is interesting that

---

[20] As the LCP group remained essentially unchanged by adding in different covariates, it raises the question of whether perhaps this is a unique grouping and the other two classes are simply artifacts one distribution that can be predicted by their covariates. Both of the models in the previous section were re-estimated by predicting the LCP group from the LCP predictors and combining the AB and AL group members into one group with the AB and AL covariates predicting the within group variation. Neither of the two class models that used the same predictors outperformed the three class models: AIC=9506.43, BIC=9627.31, Adj. BIC=9538.43, Entropy=.91; and AIC=9465.83, BIC=9603.98, Adj. BIC=9501.39, Entropy=.89, respectively. After careful examination of the model parameters and external validity of these two group models, it appears that there are, in fact, three distinct groups.

these restrictions did not significantly affect the group intercept or slope means. It did, however, shift individuals from group to group.

Table 39. Group Member Assignments: Baseline and Final Models

	Final Covariate Model Assignment		
Baseline Assignment	AL Group	LCP Group	AB Group
AL Group	65.8%	5.8%	28.3%
	N=79	N=5.8	N=34
LCP Group	3.1%	82.8%	14.1%
	N=2	N=53	N=9
AB Group	.3%	1.6%	98.1%
	N=1	N=6	N=362

After systematically reviewing each of the models, the second final covariate model was selected, which included: (1) demographic controls of gender and race, (2) LCP predictors of hyperactivity and concentration problems, (3) AL predictor of deviant peers, and (4) AB predictor of friendship importance. The model offers partial support of Moffitt's theory.

GROUP MEMBERS

While the final model that includes demographic controls has almost identical parameters to the baseline model, the class proportions were quite different. Over ten percent of the sample changed most likely trajectory group – almost all of whom went from the AL group to the AB group. The changes are due to both the addition of predictors and the additional variance restrictions. When the model was run without the predictors but with identical variance restrictions, the model was different than the one with the predictors with respect to its class proportions and parameters, so all of the differences were not due to the variance restrictions.[21] The new groups were made up of slightly different members, and this change in group membership could affect

---

[21] Three class model with equivalent variance restrictions and no predictors:
Entropy =.89, AIC=10433.22, BIC=10541.68, SSA BIC=10465.47
LCP: 10% i=3.80 (.10 fixed), s=-.30 (fixed at 0), q=.01 (fixed at 0)
AB: 80% i=1.38 (.10 fixed), s=.06 (fixed at 0), q=-.005 (fixed at 0)
AL: 10% i=1.32 (.10 fixed), s=.52 (fixed at 0), q=-.04 (fixed at 0)

the trajectory group demographics and the external validity of group membership. These differences are explored using posterior class probabilities because they control for the uncertainty of group membership and the likelihood of an individual belonging to each of the groups.

Group Demographics

Regardless of the cause of the group shift, group membership was different, and the class demographic profiles were therefore slightly altered. Using weighted posterior group-membership probabilities, a larger percentage of males made up the new AL group, and a smaller percentage of females belonged to the LCP group. The only other difference in group demographics was in race – there were significantly more Caucasians in the LCP group once the covariates and demographics were added into the model as predictors, see the comparison of trajectory group demographics below.

Table 40. Comparison of Trajectory Group Demographics

	Adolescence-Limited		Life-Course-Persistent		Adolescence-Limited	
	Baseline Model N=164	Covariate Model N=83	Baseline Model N=75	Covariate Model N=68	Baseline Model N=438	Covariate Model N=402
Sex						
Male	68.4%*	82.6%*	77.7%*	86.2%*	43.5%	42.0%
Fem	31.6%*	17.4%*	22.3%*	13.8%*	56.5%	58.0%
Race	12.4%	9.5%	18.6%*	26.8%*	13.0%	10.9%
White	87.4%	90.5%	81.4%*	73.2%*	87.0%	89.1%
Black						
Cond	38.1%	38.5%	26.9%	24.2%	31.1%	30.7%
No	30.0%	28.8%	43.3%	37.8%	33.9%	34.4%
CC	31.9%	32.7%	29.8%	38.0%	35.0%	34.8%
FSP						
Age	6.22	6.23	6.26	6.30	6.22	6.22
Inc.						
<$5K	16.4%	18.3%	21.2%	22.8%	10.2%	9.5%
$5K	18.5%	20.2%	17.5%	14.9%	16.0%	16.4%
$10K	23.1%	21.7%	20.7%	18.5%	21.8%	23.9%
$20K	18.8%	19.3%	17.1%	20.5%	20.8%	18.9%
$30K	18.4%	17.2%	14.9%	15.6%	24.4%	24.9%
$50K	4.8%	3..3%	8.5%	7.7%	6.7%	6..5%
Fam	42.7%	39.1%	36.1%	44.8%	53.4%	51.7%
2 Par	49.0%	52.8%	54.0%	46.6%	40.3%	42.4%
1 Par	7.7%	8.0%	9.5%	8.6%	5.9%	5.6%

Group Membership External Validity

One measure of external validity of group membership is how well it predicts other antisocial or delinquent behaviors. Moffitt's hypotheses about the manifestations of specific types of delinquent behavior by group (as defined by weighted posterior group-membership probabilities) were tested using different school suspension and substance use initiation rates.

With fewer individuals classified as belonging to the AL group, the difference between the groups in respect to their suspension rates was magnified when compared to the baseline model. The AL group now had an even higher suspension rate compared to the LCP and AB group. With this model, the differences between the AL and LCP groups were greater, with the AL group had a significantly higher suspension rate after the fifth grade.

Figure 37. School Suspensions Posterior Class Probability

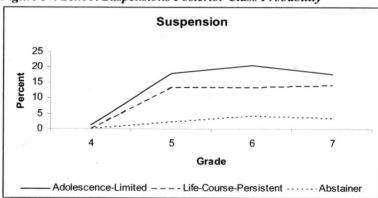

The groups were still distinctly different in their age of onset in engaging in tobacco use. The AL group now had a higher percentage that had used tobacco in sixth through twelfth grades (24%, 44%, 51%, 56%, 67%, 68%, 63% compared to 21%, 39%, 48%, 55%, 61%, 63%, 60%); however, these differences are well within a 95% Confidence Interval, and therefore, are not statistically different. The other groups followed the same pattern, with the LCP and AL groups also displaying slightly higher, but statistically equivalent tobacco initiation rates at each time point in this model.

Figure 38. **Tobacco Use Initiation by Posterior Class Probability**

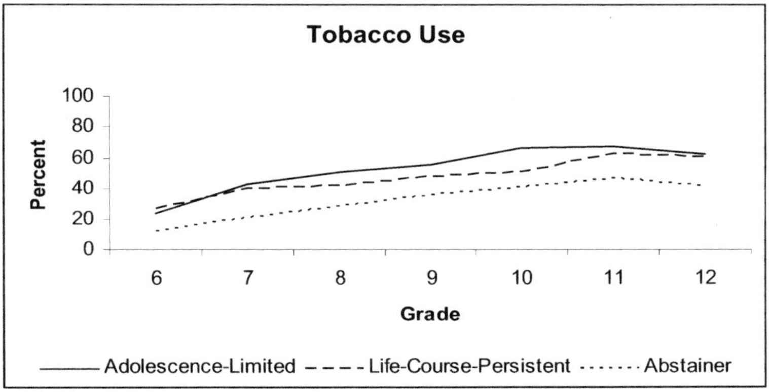

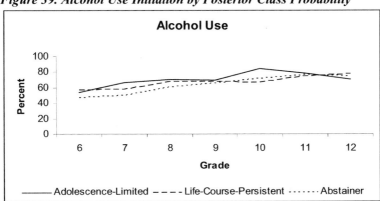

The pattern of trajectory group by alcohol use initiation was exactly the same as in the baseline model without predictors. There did not appear to be a large group difference in age of onset of drinking behavior, at least after the sixth grade, and this pattern is statistically identical to the one uncovered in the baseline model.

Figure 39. **Alcohol Use Initiation by Posterior Class Probability**

After adding the predictors of class membership, the patterns of marijuana use age of initiation did not change a great deal between the trajectory classes. The AB group did experience an increase of group members reporting marijuana experimentation at a younger age and overall. At each time period except for in the sixth grade, there was a significantly larger percentage of AL group members reporting having tried marijuana in this model than in the baseline model. The differences in the other groups were not statistically significant.

Figure 40. Marijuana Use by Posterior Class Probability

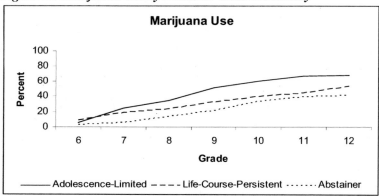

The difference in the pattern of trajectory group by illicit drug use initiation was minimal when comparing the baseline model to the one with predictors. It appears that the AL group begins experimenting with illicit drugs at a younger age and at higher rates when it was defined in the predictor model than the baseline model (9%, 31%, 41%, 51%, 60%, 68%, 68% compared to 10%, 26%, 38%, 47%, 55%, 62%, 61% in the baseline model), but these differences were only significant in tenth through twelfth grades. The other two groups had the age of onset for illicit drug use in the baseline and covariate models.

There were no differences in age of onset for experimentation with any drugs between the baseline and the covariate models. The pattern of age of initiation between the trajectory classes was identical to the model without predictors, which shows very little difference between the groups. Trajectory group membership was not as a good predictor of when an individual will begin experimenting with both legal and illegal drugs as it is predicting who will use tobacco, marijuana, and other illegal drugs.

Figure 41. Illicit Drug Use by Posterior Class Probability

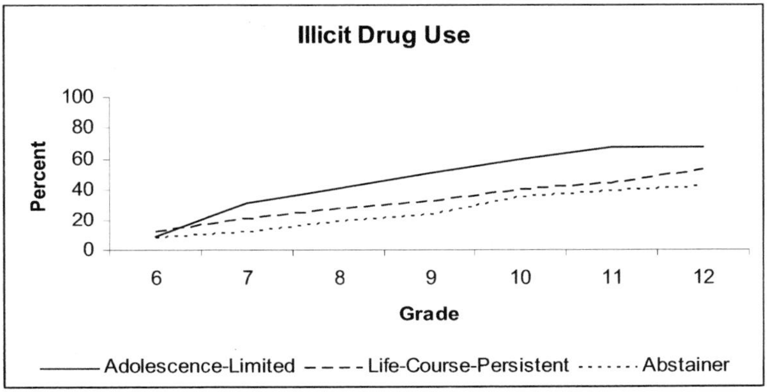

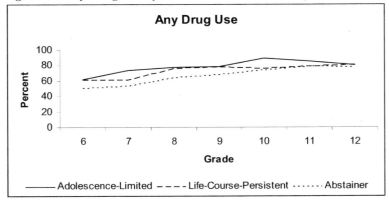

Figure 42. Any Drug Use by Posterior Class Probability

SUMMARY

The patterns of suspension and tobacco, alcohol, and other drug use initiation for the groups defined by a three group model with covariates and demographic controls were almost identical to those of the baseline three group model. The AL group lost members in this model (n=136 compared to n=164), and those who remained had slightly higher rates of suspension, and tobacco, and substance use initiation rates. The new distribution of group members did not impact the rates in either the AB or LCP groups for any of the concurrent indicators of delinquency.

This chapter brought all the predictors into one final model to test Moffitt's predictors of group membership. Gender, race, concentration problems, hyperactivity, peer deviance, and friendship importance were all significant predictors of trajectory group membership. When the predictors were added to the model, group membership and the trajectory shapes changed considerably.

When they were added without demographic controls, the fewest restrictions were placed on the model. In this model, the three groups displayed very different group trajectories during elementary school, but the LCP and AL groups appeared to be following identical trajectories through middle and high schools. In this model, unlike the baseline model without predictors, the trajectory groups never cross, and the class proportions were different as well (AB: 64.5% to 57%, AL: 24.4% to 31%, and LCP: 11.1% to 12%). It is interesting that adding predictors shifted AB group members into the AL group, but left the LCP group virtually unchanged

Adding in all the predictors and the demographic controls necessitated more restrictions to be placed on the model for it to converge. This slightly changes both the theoretical and empirical meaning of the groups, and could be responsible for some of the differences in the models. When gender and race were added to the model as predictors of group, the shapes of the trajectories were altered along with the class proportions. The groups now crossed in late elementary school, meaning that the AL group actually exhibited higher delinquency scores than the LCP group upon entrance to middle school, and remained higher throughout high school After adding these variance restrictions and the demographic predictors, the LCP group membership remained the same, but this time more people were switched from the AL group to the AB group (AB: 64.5% to 73%, AL: 24.4% to 15%).

The other relationships were all in the directions anticipated by Moffitt's theory, regardless of the presence of demographic controls or model restrictions. The higher the teacher's rating of concentration problems and hyperactivity, the more likely an individual belonged to the LCP group than either the AB or AL group. LCP group members appeared to have higher scores on peer deviance than AB group members, but they were statistically equivalent to the AL group members. Depending on whether demographic controls are included in the model, AL group members could be predicted by either concentration problems or hyperactivity from AB group members, which is contrary to Moffitt's hypothesis. Neighborhood deviance was no longer a significant predictor of group membership once other variables were controlled for. And finally, friendship importance did differentiate AB group members from AL group members. Overall, there is support for her many of her hypotheses, but not all of them.

CHAPTER 9.

Discussion and Conclusions

This study sought to test one of the major developmental theories of crime, Moffitt's taxonomy, which explains the age-crime curve using subgroups with different developmental trajectories of delinquent behavior. She hypothesized that there are distinct groups of offenders, each with its own etiology and different developmental trajectories of offending (Moffitt, 1993). Theoretically, the most striking difference between the types of offenders is the stability of antisocial behavior across age and situation.

Life-course-persistent offenders begin their antisocial behavior at a young age and continue to offend throughout their lives. This study found a small group that began displaying antisocial behavior at a young age, but this behavior appeared to decline over time. *Adolescence-limited* offenders are involved in criminal behavior only through their adolescent years, and are primarily responsible for the peak of the age-crime curve in adolescence. This study found a group of individuals who increased in antisocial behavior through middle school, as anticipated by the theory; however, it is premature to claim that this group desisted in adulthood as there is no data on this time period. A final group of abstainers was also found in this study, but the group was much larger than Moffitt anticipated.

Theoretically, the two types of offenders have very different developmental trajectories and causal factors. Life-course-persistent offenders begin to display antisocial behavior in infancy or childhood because of a confluence of psycho-physiological factors and environmental deviance. Adolescence-limited offenders do not begin to exhibit deviant behavior until adolescence and mimic the antisocial behavior they observe in their peers to gain social recognition. This study did find evidence that there are different sets of factors that can predict the different trajectory groups, and in general, they were congruent with Moffitt's theory.

The following chapter summarizes and discusses the findings from the previous four chapters that tested some of Moffitt's hypotheses about the manifestations of antisocial behavior over time using data collected from a sample of children in Baltimore, MD. The research questions and hypotheses are reviewed and evaluated considering all the results from the study: (1) are their "groups" of developmental trajectories, as Moffitt has suggested, (2) do these "groups" follow Moffitt's anticipated patterns regarding the shapes of the developmental trajectories and class proportions, and (3) are Moffitt's predictors of group membership empirically sound. These questions were explored using a relatively new statistical technique, group-based trajectory modeling, which was also examined.

DO THE DATA SUPPORT MOFFITT'S THEORY REGARDING THE DIFFERENTIAL MANIFESTATIONS OF ANTISOCIAL BEHAVIOR?

The study found clear results that group-based trajectory modeling outperformed the traditional growth curve modeling. Regardless of how the groups were defined, each of the models captured the heterogeneity in growth trajectories better than a single class growth model, which assumes that trajectories are based on growth factors that follow a normal distribution that can be predicted in a manner similar to a multiple regression. It was evident that modeling a multinomial latent process above the underlying growth processes improved the overall accuracy of the model. The fact that multiple group models fit the data better than a single group model supports Moffitt's hypothesis that there are distinct groups of trajectories and the conceptualization of a taxonomy of delinquency is empirically sound.

One of the important theoretical and methodological issues when considering a group-based trajectory model is how to define group membership. Some researchers believe that a group should constitute a relatively homogeneous group within a heterogeneous population (Nagin, 2005), while others believe that smaller heterogeneous populations make up the larger heterogeneous population (Fuzhong, Duncan, Duncan, & Acock, 2001; Muthén, 2000; Schafer et al., 2003). This study took an empirical approach to answer the question of how a group should be defined. Each of the different ways in which the variance in the latent growth factors could be defined was explored. Five variance structures were considered:

1. No variance in the intercept or slope.
2. Allowing variance in the intercept and slope factors, but constraining them to be equal across class, also known as variance invariance.

3. Allowing the variance in the intercept factor to vary across class, but fixing the slope variance to be equal across class.
4. Allowing the slope variance to differ across class, but fixing the intercept variance to remain constant across class.
5. Allowing both the intercept and slope variances to differ across classes.

The five different structures change the meaning of group membership by determining how similar group members must be with respect to their developmental trajectories. Using the first structure without variation in intercept or the slope factors, the most restrictive set of models was estimated. When there was no variation in the latent growth factors, the latent classes are assumed to be made up of homogeneous subgroups of the population. Under this assumption, a greater number of groups were needed to capture the variation in trajectories because group members are supposed to be the same, with only random error around the group means. Group members were as similar as possible, and therefore according to some researchers, it is the most meaningful conceptualization of a group (Nagin, 2005). When this set of models was estimated, a four group model was selected as the best fit, which was comprised of: (1) an abstainer group, (2) a high but declining group, (3) a low adolescence-limited group, and (4) a high adolescence-limited group.

The second latent variance structure that was investigated allowed within group variance, but placed major restrictions on that variance. The within class variance was constrained to be equal across classes. Basically this is a method of allowing group members to vary in their intercepts and slopes while keeping the structure of a "group" as comparable as possible across latent classes. A group now is made up of a heterogeneous group of individuals, instead of a homogeneous group of individuals as with the previous set of models.

Modeling in the variation allowed diversity between the group members, and the questions become how heterogeneous is the group and does group membership still have any meaning. By constraining the variance to be equal between groups, or requiring variance invariance, each of the groups is as heterogeneous as the others. Group members were allowed to vary around the group mean intercept and slope, but the variation within each of the groups will be equal. Under these variance assumptions, a three group model was found to be the best fit. Allowing the individuals to vary around their group averages eliminated the need for an additional trajectory group. The change in assumptions both increased and reduced the complexity of the model; one group was eliminated, but now variances around the intercept and slope factors were estimated. In total, the four class model estimated the same number of parameters and the three class models that estimated equal variation in the intercept and slope factors between groups.

The third and fourth variance structures constrained one of the latent constructs' variance to be equal across groups and allowed the other to differ. Basically, these models allowed the groups to be more or less heterogeneous than the previous models in two distinctive ways. The first allowed some groups to be more heterogeneous with respect to their intercepts. When variance was allowed to be estimated for each group, the group that most closely approximates the adolescence-limited group had a greater variation in its intercepts than the other two groups. In the second model, when variance was allowed to vary in the slope factors across classes, the same adolescence-limited group was found to have greater variation than the other two groups. In both of these variance structures, three class models best fit the data.

The final variance structure that was explored allowed both the variance in the latent intercept and slope factors to vary across groups. This was the most complex model because it required the estimation of more parameters than any of the previous models. A three group model was still found to be the best fitting model. Allowing variance to be estimated within and between groups, latent classes are now a mix of individuals, with some being more heterogeneous than others. A major question with allowing this much variation, especially between groups so that each group is not even representing an equally heterogeneous group, is whether or not groups are meaningful. This study found that estimating the variances between and within group independently resulted in a better fitting model, with two of the groups (high declining group/life-course-persistent and abstainer) being more homogeneous than the third group (adolescence-limited).

The most important lesson from comparing the different variance assumptions was that once variance was allowed within groups, a three class model was always the best fit. This supports the conclusion that a three class model is a reliable finding and not simply an artifact of how the latent variances are defined.

Another important finding was that once variance was allowed to be estimated separately within group in either or both the latent constructs, the parameter estimates were statistically equivalent. The same results were produced when the intercept variance, slope variance, or intercept and slope variance, were freed to vary between classes. These estimates were slightly different from the model in which the variances of both parameters were fixed to be equal. This appears to be because the adolescence-limited group had more variation in its group members' individual trajectories, which can be seen in the spaghetti plots. This fits with Moffitt's theory, as adolescence-limited offenders are highly influenced by environmental factors, display delinquency to gain social recognition, and only act out while there is a disparity between their physical and social maturity (which would vary by individual), all of which would make this group much more heterogeneous.

While this is an interesting empirical finding, it is also a very significant theoretical finding. The way in which latent variable constructs are defined produces groups that have different meanings, and these different meanings could influence the external validity of group membership. The final model selected defined groups as clusters of similar developmental trajectories, but each group had its own distribution of latent growth factors. This model was a theoretically better fit because Moffitt's theory implies that the adolescence-limited group will display more variation, as they are a more diverse group of individuals who are acting out in order to gain social acknowledgment after reaching physical maturity yet not achieving social maturity. There will be substantial individual differences in ages of physical and social maturity which would make this group more heterogeneous than the groups that either always or never engages in delinquent behavior (life-course-persistents and abstainers, respectively). By allowing varying variances, the model is essentially allowing this group to vary more and allowing the other groups to remain relatively homogenous, as is implied in Moffitt's taxonomy. It was concluded that modeling in unequal variation across groups is the most theoretically and empirically sound definition of her groups.

With the advancement in modeling theory and statistical software in group-based trajectory modeling, it is now possible manipulate models in very complex ways. This is a remarkable case of a methodology being developed to answer a theoretical question that has, in turn, outpaced the theory. What began as a practice inspired by theory became a technique that has surpassed theory in its sophistication and methodological decisions are being dictated by empirical instead of theoretical appropriateness. It should be noted that this study only explored a narrow range of modeling options available to developmental theorists and almost every conceivable combination of variance restrictions and population distributions can now be estimated. For examples of some of the more complex models, such as the non-parametric growth mixture models, see Kreuter & Muthén, 2008. These options challenge criminologists to think creativity and it is important that model selection is based on theory and not solely on the empirical fit.

Allowing variation within and/or between groups also opens modeling opportunities that are not possible with the traditional models that do not specify variation. With these more complex models, differences within groups can be explored and there is great potential for theory growth and integration. While covariates can predict group membership using any of the models presented in this paper, only those with estimated variance can include mediating effects and explore within group differences. Using these models, one set of covariates may predict group membership, while a completely different set may be related to differences in intercept or slope within groups. The modeling opportunities are almost endless, which yet again emphasizes that the statistical methods currently available may be more advanced than the theories that are being tested.

This study found evidence that exploring the latent variance structures is a worthwhile research endeavor. These very small and technical differences had significant implications on class enumeration, proportions, class membership, and trajectory shapes. Theory should always guide hypothesis testing, and in this case, it made theoretical sense to explore the within and between group variance, which has been, up until this point, regularly neglected in the criminological literature. This study demonstrates that a minor technical issue is meaningful, both empirically and theoretically, and that it should be considered and explored in future research.

DO THE DIFFERENT GROUPS FOLLOW THE ANTICIPATED PATTERNS OF MOFFITT'S THEORY?

Number of Groups

Moffitt hypothesized there would be three distinct groups – a group that was always delinquent, regardless of age or environment (LCP), a group that is delinquent during adolescence (AL), and a third group who is never delinquent (AB). If her theory is correct, a three group model should be empirically superior to models that have other numbers of groups.

This study found a four group model when there was no within group variance and three group models when the variance restrictions were loosened. Although some studies of antisocial behavior have found three group models (e.g., Brame, Mulvey, & Piquero, 2001; Broidy et al., 2003; Bushway, Brame, & Paternoster, 1999; Lancourse et al., 2003; Maughan et al., 2000; Paternoster, Brame, & Farrington, 2001; Tremblay et al., 2004), the majority of group-based trajectory modeling research on antisocial or criminal behavior have uncovered between four and six distinct groups (e.g., Bonger, Koot, van der Ende, & Verhulst, 2004; Broidy et. al, 2003; Bushway, Thronberry, & Krohn, 2003; D'Unger, Land, McCall, & Nagin, 1998; Fergusson & Horwood, 2002; Moffitt, 2006; Nagin, 2005; Nagin, Farringon, & Moffitt, 1995; Nagin & Land, 1993; Lacourse, et al., 2003; Nagin & Tremblay, 2001a; Nagin & Tremblay, 2001b; Piquero, Brame, Mazerolle, & Haapanen, 2002; Sampson & Laub, 2005a; White, Bates & Buyske, 2001). It is important to note that models are not necessarily comparable across studies because of differences in sample, time frame, dependent variable, and model definition.

Many of the aforementioned studies used samples that are quite different from the Baltimore data used for this study. For instance, some group-based trajectory studies use samples consisting exclusively of offenders, which would totally eliminate and/or severely limit the inclusion of members from the abstainer group. These studies also include a variety of age groups and ranges, with studies that focus strictly on infancy, childhood, adolescence, adulthood, and different combinations of all four. The present study included childhood and adolescence, but stopped at the entry to adulthood. Different time frames have produced a different number of trajectory groups, with longer time frames generally uncovering more distinct trajectory classes (Broidy et al., 2003; Eggleston, Laub, & Sampson, 2003; Piquero, 2008).

Another notable difference was in the behavior that was the main interest of the study, as some examined official arrest and conviction data, some self-report, and still others using teacher and parent ratings of delinquent behavior. Researchers have found that self-report data is much richer and therefore more variation can be extracted and modeled than official data, which results in different numbers of trajectory classes, shapes, and proportions (Nagin, Farrington, & Moffitt, 1995). More trajectory groups are usually uncovered when using self-, teacher-, or parent-report behavior than using official reports of criminal behavior (Broidy et al., 2003; Piquero, 2008). While it can be argued that these are proxies of the same underlying construct, there are large differences between them. This study used the TOCA-R Aggression/Disruption Subscale, which may represent something different from the measures used in previous studies.

In addition to these important differences between previous research and the current study, the variances in the latent variables were defined in different ways. This study has demonstrated that by allowing variation in the latent growth factors, a different number of groups is necessary to capture the heterogeneity in growth trajectories, which is another prominent difference between this study and most of the published studies using group-based trajectory modeling. The models described in this study that allow variance in the latent growth factors are more complex models and estimate many more parameters than most of the studies have considered in the past. As the models become more complex and allow more variation, fewer classes are necessary, and this could be why this study found a three group model to be the best fit.

Shape of the Trajectories

Moffitt's taxonomy includes specific hypotheses about the shapes of the three developmental trajectory groups. The abstainers should have little to no variation from a null growth model. The adolescent-limited group should increase in their delinquency in adolescence and decrease into and through adulthood. And finally, Moffitt's taxonomy hypothesizes that life-course-persistent offenders will display high rates of delinquency starting at a young age and continuing through adulthood. The life-course-persistent and adolescence-limited offender group trajectories may cross and change relative positions in adolescence, when the AL group should be offending at the highest rate.

Moffitt provided no absolutes about the level of delinquency exhibited by any group, only their relative positions. Another important note about trajectory shape is that it is highly dependent on the number of trajectories modeled as well as the dependent variable.

Therefore, it is virtually impossible to compare the shapes of the trajectories across studies since they are all modeled on different scales. The most that can be reliably evaluated across studies is whether they increase, decrease, remain stable, and/or exhibit a quadratic function. In this section, the trajectories derived in the baseline model (model without predictors) will be compared to those predicted by Moffitt's theory. The trajectories for all of the three class models were statistically equivalent, which is why only one model is being shown here.

The life-course-persistent group should begin high and remain high in antisocial behavior throughout their lives, as they should display antisocial behavior across time and situation. Moffitt did not make any precise predictions about the exact level of antisocial behavior, only that it would be higher than the other groups (except for perhaps during adolescence). This study did find a group that displayed a higher level of delinquency in the classroom; however, the group did not remain high. The group intercept was three times higher than the other groups (3.67 compared to 1.26 and 1.36) and this was also the only group that had a negative slope (mean slope=-.32). It should be noted that this is not the first study to find a group that followed this pattern (Broidy et al., 2003; Lancourse et al., 2005).

Although this negative slope appears to refute Moffitt's theory, there are several methodological and theoretical explanations to explain this phenomenon that do not necessarily counter her theory. The methodological issue relates to the assessment of delinquency. It is possible that the measurement used does not appropriately capture delinquency across childhood and adolescence equally. According to Life Course/Social Field Theory, the classroom is no longer the dominant social field in adolescence, and therefore using a teacher-rating during this time period may not accurately capture delinquent behavior. In middle and high school, peers are theoretically more appropriate raters of delinquent behavior. This problem should be minimized for this trajectory group because according to Moffitt, life-course-persistent offenders should be antisocial across time and environment, and consequently would be assumed to be exhibiting higher levels of antisocial behavior in the classroom as well as all other situations.

Figure 43. *Life-Course-Persistent Group Sample Means*

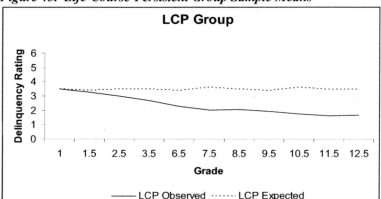

The theoretical justification for the discrepancy between Moffitt's prediction and these findings are that the life-course-persistent group members either could have learned to conform their behavior in the classroom or dropped out of school. Although initial ratings of aggression/disruption were not associated with missing data at any one data collection point, it is possible that there is a multivariate pattern of missing data or another related variable could account for life-course-persistent drop out. A study conducted by the Economic Policy Institute conducted in the years that this sample should have graduated; Baltimore City Public Schools have the second lowest graduation rate in the country, with only 38.5% of the students graduating on time (Mishel & Roy, 2006). One source of the missing data in this study is school drop out, which could be associated with higher delinquency and would therefore alter the class proportion and trajectory shape of the life-course-persistent group. However, this is less likely, as it was found that trajectory group and missing data are not related. It is interesting to note that this study followed a higher percentage of students through high school than the area average who graduated (55.4% of the sample was interviewed in twelfth grade compared to the 38.5% graduation rate).

The adolescence-limited group should display low levels of delinquency in childhood and then increase rapidly into and through adolescence. As group members begin to experience social maturity and independence, they should begin desisting from delinquent behavior. In this study, there was a group that approximates Moffitt's adolescence-limited group.

Figure 44. Adolescence-Limited Group Sample Means

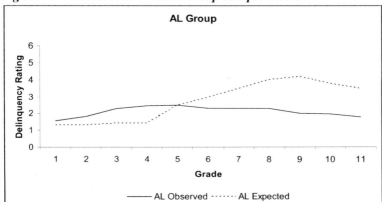

This group began at the same place as the abstainer group, as anticipated by the theory. The adolescence-limited group does increase through adolescence, but it is not a dramatic increase (slope mean=.30, which declines from quadratic term=-.02) as anticipated by the theory. Additionally, it appears that the delinquency ratings peak in the beginning of adolescence (sixth grade, Mean=2.5) and decrease before the end of adolescence. The last data collection period available for this sample was in twelfth grade, so it impossible to know if this group will desist from delinquent behavior or continue on a different track. At this end of the study, they displayed the highest delinquency ratings, as anticipated by Moffitt. Again, it must be recognized that the discrepancy between the observed and expected trajectories could be due to data and methodological limitations.

The abstainer group was hypothesized to exhibit an approximately null growth mode because the members should never display delinquent behavior. This study found evidence of an abstainer group, although its trajectory was not exactly as Moffitt predicted. This group always displayed the lowest delinquency ratings, but their delinquency scores were always significantly higher than zero. They also did experience a very small increase in delinquency scores over time (slope mean=.04). The shape of the abstainer group's trajectory is the closest to Moffitt's predictions.

Figure 45. Abstainer Group Sample Means

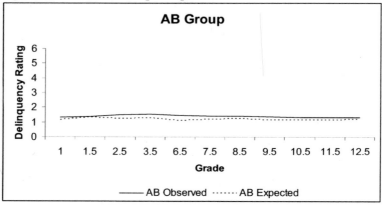

Overall, the shapes of the trajectories are not quite what would be anticipated by Moffitt's theory. The closest trajectory to the life-course-offender group appeared to be more accurately characterized as a high declining group. Her theory does not anticipate such a large negative slope, although a negative slope is not necessarily contrary to her theory as she never eliminated the possibility of an independent age effect. The adolescence-limited group also peaked at a much younger age than was anticipated. Again, it is possible that this early peak is an artifact from study and school drop-out, as those displaying higher rates of delinquent behavior may be more likely to drop out of school or be absent on the day in which the assessment was collected. It is also possible that the data limitations are responsible for the discrepancies because the delinquency measure only applied to the classroom, which was only the dominant social field in childhood and becomes less prominent in adolescence.

It is interesting to note that the life-course-persistent and adolescence-limited group mean trajectories actually cross one another, which has not been found in other studies (Broidy et al., 2003), but is anticipated by Moffitt's theory. She hypothesized that in adolescence, adolescence-limited and life-course-persistent offenders will begin to look alike, because more and more adolescence-limited group members should begin offending. This hypothesis was confirmed in all of the three group models, regardless of how the models were specified.

Class Proportions

Moffitt also offered hypotheses about the proportions of individuals that should belong to each of the trajectory groups. As adolescence-limited delinquency is supposed to be a normative behavior, the majority of the sample should follow this pattern. Life-course-persistent offending should be a statistically aberrant phenomenon, with only approximately five to eight percent of the population belonging to this group. Moffitt also predicted that abstaining from delinquency is unusual as well, although she did not offer any concrete hypotheses about the exact size of this group.

Moffitt hypothesized that approximately five to eight percent of the general population would belong to the life-course-persistent group. This study found roughly 11% of the population followed the life-course-persistent pattern, as defined by weighted posterior group-membership probabilities. Other studies have found between four and eleven percent of males and two to ten percent of females follow a relatively high delinquency pattern (Broidy et al., 2003; D'Unger, Lancourse et. al., 2003; Land, & McCall; Kratzer & Hodgins, 1999). The proportion of the sample that belonged to the high group was the only one that remained stable regardless of how the model was defined. The fact that a larger percentage of the proportion of this sample followed this pattern than was anticipated by Moffitt could be because the sample used for this study is from a high-risk area, and it would therefore follow that there would be a higher percentage of life-course-persistent offenders.

The adolescence-limited group should be composed of the majority of the sample, as Moffitt predicted that adolescence-limited delinquency is normative. This study found between 9.3% and 24.4% of the sample in the baseline models depending on the model restrictions, and 15% to 41% of the sample in the models that included predictors belonged to the AL group. The differences in the class proportions are mainly based on the way in which the variation in the latent constructs is defined. The final models that were selected found the adolescence-limited group was between 15% and 25% of the sample, which is still much lower than anticipated by Moffitt's theory. However, other studies have found approximately the same proportion in the middle trajectory group, anywhere from between 22% and 31% (Broidy et al., 2003).

The final group, the abstainers, should be statistically anomalous, according to the theory. This study, however, found this group to be, by far, the most common trajectory pattern. Between 65% and 81% of the sample in the baseline models and 49% and 73% of the sample in the prediction models belonged to the abstainer group, depending on how the variance was structured. The final models estimate that 65% of the sample in the baseline and 74% of the sample in the prediction model belong to the abstaining trajectory group. This is a far greater proportion than anticipated by Moffitt's theory, which posits that a very small proportion should follow this pattern. Previous studies have found similar abstainer class proportions, ranging from 38% to 80% (Broidy et al., 2003; D'Unger, Lancourse et al., 2003; Land, & McCall, 2002; Maughan et al., 2000).

Overall, the class proportions do not support Moffitt's theory. They are very different from what she hypothesized for the abstainer and adolescence-limited groups, but it is much closer to what she hypothesized for the life-course-persistent group. Notably, the highest group (which most closely approximately the life-course-persistent group) is immutable to change when modifying variance restrictions while the other groups are highly malleable. The differences in class proportions across models are quite large, and it is clear that the way a model is defined highly influences class proportions. Most previous studies use the most restrictive models, which in this study, appears to produce and overestimation of the abstainer class proportion.

External Validity of Group Membership

Since the validity and reliability of trajectory group membership is at the center of a current dispute among criminologists, the validity of group membership is exceptionally important. Differences between trajectory group members on alternative measures of delinquency, such as suspension rates, alcohol, tobacco, marijuana, and other drug use initiation, were used to test whether group membership is meaningful. For the most part, Moffitt's predictions were confirmed in both the baseline and predictor models. Abstainer group members reported nonparticipation from all substance use for the longest and the adolescence-limited group had a younger average age of onset and a larger percent of its group members experimenting with cigarettes, alcohol, marijuana, and illicit drugs. However, the differences in group initiation rates were not tremendously large.

While these findings provide some support Moffitt's theory, they are far from irrefutable evidence of the external validity of trajectory groups. For example, a much higher percentage of the abstainers were experimenting with substances, such as tobacco, alcohol, marijuana, and illicit drugs, than would be expected by her taxonomy. Also, while the adolescence-limited group did have a lower initiation age into experimentation with illegal substances and a greater percentage of group members reporting experimentation, it was not always significantly different from the other groups (e.g., alcohol use). The external validity of group membership is questionable at this point – while trajectory group does appear to predict suspension, tobacco and drug initiation rates, the differences are not as great as would be expected if group membership was a large predictor of alternative delinquent behavior.

DO THE DATA SUPPORT MOFFITT'S HYPOTHESES REGARDING THE ETIOLOGIES OF THE DIFFERENT DELINQUENCY TRAJECTORIES?

Moffitt makes the following predictions about the etiologies of the trajectory groups:

1. The life-course-persistent group will show evidence of early behavioral problems across multiple domains, early psycho-physiological problems, and environmental and/or contextual dysfunction, such as parenting problems.
2. The adolescence-limited group should parallel the abstainer group in the manifestation of childhood behavioral problems, but differ from them in their experiences with the maturity gap and access to deviant peer role models.
3. The abstainer group may show evidence of some resilience factor that is preventing the members from engaging in antisocial or delinquent behavior, such as involvement with positive peers and social recognition.

Her hypotheses about the characteristics of the life-course-persistent, adolescence-limited, and abstainer groups were entered into separate models to determine whether they predicted group membership. The predictors were also added in three ways in order to determine empirically how they influence delinquency:

1. Predictors of a general growth model to test whether the predictors are simply explaining the variance in the intercept and slope factors, which would mean group-based trajectory modeling is only capturing artificial cutoffs in a normal distribution.
2. Predictors of group membership.
3. Predictors of within class variability.

In each case, the model fit increased the most when adding the covariates as predictors of class, as is anticipated by the theory. The results provided partial support for Moffitt's hypotheses. In each model, the predictors relate to group membership better than a general growth model or within class variability, as anticipated by her theory. This offers further empirical support that group membership has validity. The abstainer model found that friendship importance was a significant predictor of abstaining from delinquency, and could differentiate between abstainers and adolescence-limited offenders. The adolescence-limited model found that both exposure to deviant peers and living in a neighborhood that is perceived to be more criminogenic significantly predicted group membership in the direction that Moffitt suggested. The mental health and parenting measurements were not significant predictors of life-course-persistent group membership, but higher levels of concentration problems and hyperactivity were associated with both the life-course-persistent and adolescence-limited groups.

Table 41. Summary of Significant Predictors of Group Membership

	AB Model	AL Model	LCP Model	Full Model	Full Model with Demographic Controls
Friendship Importance	✓			✓	✓
Peer Deviance		✓		✓	✓
Neighborhood Deviance		✓			
Concentration			✓	✓	✓
Hyperactivity			✓	✓	✓

Taken together, the results provide support for Moffitt's hypotheses. The abstainers and adolescence-limited models found relationships that were anticipated by her theory. Deviant peers and neighborhoods differentiated abstainers from adolescence-limited offenders, but deviant peers also distinguished abstainers from life-course-persistent offenders, which were not specifically projected by Moffitt's theory.

The largest discrepancy between the theory and the findings from these analyses was in the life-course-persistent model. Several of the variables that Moffitt predicted would be associated with life-course-persistent offending were found to be insignificant (psychological dysfunction measured by depression and anxiety, and environmental dysfunction measured by parental monitoring and parental discipline). Even more troubling with respect to her taxonomy was the relationship between concentration problems and hyperactivity and adolescence-limiting offending. According to her theory, there should be no difference between abstainer and adolescence-limited group members on these variables, but these analyses did find a significant relationship. It appears that concentration problems and hyperactivity distinguish abstainer group members from both adolescence-limited and life-course-persistent group members, which is problematic because it suggests that it may not simply experiences with the maturity gap that are driving adolescence-limited offenders into displaying antisocial behavior during adolescence.

Adding in all the predictors and the demographic controls necessitated more restrictions to be placed on the model for convergence problems. This slightly changed both the theoretical and empirical meaning of the groups, and could be responsible for some of the differences between the models.[22] When gender and race were added to the model as predictors of group, the shapes of the trajectories were altered along with the class proportions. The groups now crossed in late elementary school, meaning that the adolescence-limited group actually exhibited higher delinquency scores than the life-course-persistent group upon entrance to middle school, and remained higher

---

[22] The different models required fixing the variance of the intercept factors to be equal and the variance in the slope factors to be zero. Changing the latent variance structure of the models was not responsible for all of the differences in the estimated model parameters, as simply adding these restrictions into a model with no predictors did not produce this change. Therefore, it appears that the differences between the full model with predictors and the baseline model is due in part to differences in model restrictions and in part due to the addition of predictors.

throughout high school. After adding these variance restrictions and the demographic predictors, the life-course-persistent group membership remained the same, but this time more subjects switched from the adolescence-limited group to the abstainer group (AB: 64.5% to 73%, AL: 24.4% to 15%).

The significant relationships were all in the direction anticipated by Moffitt's theory, regardless of the presence of demographic controls or model restrictions. Concentration problems and hyperactivity appear to increase the likelihood of an individual belonged to the life-course-persistent group than the abstainer or adolescence-limited group, as has been found in other studies (Bartusch, Lynam, Moffitt, & Silva, 1997; Herrenkohl et al., 2000; Moffitt, 1990; Raine et al., 2005; Shaw, Lacourse, & Nagin, 2005). Life-course-persistent and adolescence-limited group members had higher scores on peer deviance than abstainer group members but their scores are statistically equivalent to one another, which has not been found in other studies (Bartusch, Lynam, Moffitt, & Silva, 1997). Adolescence-limited group members can be differentiated on concentration problems and hyperactivity in childhood from abstainer group members, which contradicts Moffitt's theory. Neighborhood deviance was no longer a significant predictor of group membership once other variables are controlled. And finally, friendship importance did differentiate abstainer group members from adolescence-limited group members. Overall, there is support for her many of her hypotheses, but not all of them.

Table 42. Summary of Predictors on Group Membership

	AL vs. AB	AL vs. LCP	AL vs LCP
Concentration	0	+	–
Hyperactivity	+	+	–
Peer Deviance	+	+	0
Friendship	–	0	0

The predictors of group membership can be conceptualized as risk factors, or variables that increase or decrease the probability of belonging to any group. This study found that high teacher ratings of hyperactivity and concentration problems in childhood predicted life-course-persistent group membership (although, at this point, there is not enough data to support that they will continue to display differential antisocial behavior into or throughout adulthood). It also appears that moderate levels of hyperactivity increase the risk that someone will follow the adolescence-limited group trajectory. These findings are similar to those found in previous studies (Laub, Nagin, & Sampson, 1998; Kjelsberg, 1999; Maughan et al., 2000; Moffitt, 1993). Deviant peers in middle school are a risk factor for belonging to either the life-course-persistent or the adolescence-limited groups. Strong bonds to friends appear to be a protective factor from the adolescence-limited group, as has been found in previous studies (Piquero, Brezina, & Turner, 2005), but there is no difference between abstainers and life-course-persistent offenders on this predictor.

This has interesting implications for prevention and intervention programming. It points to targeting children displaying hyperactivity and concentration problem, as these problems predict long term behavioral patterns. This is an important finding because teacher ratings appear to be a valid measure to identify those at risk and would not be difficult or expensive to collect. The finding that deviant peers in middle school are risk factor for higher delinquency trajectories can help identify those at risk through their friend networks. Programs can target individuals with delinquent friend groups, or even aim to prevent these friendships from forming prior to adolescence. Finally, it does appear that a strong belief in friendship acts as a protective factor, which could be built in as a component of a prevention/intervention program. Research validated risk and protective factors are essential for successful prevention and intervention programming, and this study highlighted several that had been established in previous research studies.

STRENGTHS AND LIMITATIONS

Before drawing any concrete conclusions, it is necessary to revisit some of the limitations of the study so that they results can be put in context. No study is without flaws, and these must be considered when interpreting the results. This study also possesses some important strengths that allowed it to investigate phenomenon that have yet to be explored in the criminological literature. The strengths and limitations of this study fall into the following categories: (1) sample, (2) measurement, and (3) statistical.

Sample

The main limitation with the sample used in this study involves its generalizability. This study used an epidemiologically-defined sample of students from Baltimore, MD. Using this type of sample is a great strength of this study because the selection biases associated with other selection criteria are avoided; however, it captures only one community which may not be generliazable to the entire population, or even other similar communities.

Another issue with the sample is the length of time for which they have been followed. This project began observing the sample in the fall of first grade in 1993, and data are only available through twelfth grade currently (collected in the Spring of 2005), which limits the ability to test Moffitt's theory, as the adolescence-limited youths should just begin to age out of crime at this point. It also prevents testing whether the groups predict criminal behavior into and through adulthood. In short, there is no ability to test whether the adolescence-limited group actually desists from crime in adulthood, if the life-course-persistent offenders continue to offend, or if the abstainers remain abstinent throughout adulthood.

Finally, as with any longitudinal study, missing data are problematic. Missingness at the later data collection points and study drop-out can be related to the phenomenon of interest, in this case delinquency. This study assumed data to be missing at random (MAR) because previous analyses reported that missing data was not related to teacher ratings, academic achievement, race/ethnicity, sex, or free lunch status in the first few years of data collection (Furr-Holden et al., 2004). These analyses also found no bivariate relationship between missing data and aggression in either of the first grade measurement periods. However, it is still a possibility that missing data biased the results.

Although the sample clearly presents limitations, it is also one of the greatest strengths of this study because it was drawn from the general population, and is therefore appropriate to test Moffitt's theory. Many of the previous studies that have examined taxonomies use offender samples, which theoretically should not include the abstainer group, and are not the most appropriate for testing her particular theory (Francis et al., 2004; Laub et al., 1998; Sampson & Laub, 2003; Piquero et al., 2002). There have been several other longitudinal general population and birth cohort studies that have employed group-based trajectory modeling to examine taxonomies, but none of them are as contemporary sample as the 1993 Baltimore sample (Dunedin Health and Human Development Studies (1972), Cambridge Study in Delinquent Development (1961), Philadelphia Birth Cohort Study (1958), Pittsburgh Youth Study (1987), Rochester Youth Development Study (1988)). While using such a contemporary sample limits the ability to test Moffitt's theory through adulthood, it does provide a more current picture of delinquency at the present time, which may or may not match historical samples.

Measurement

Limitations with measurement are a common problem in research. In this study, the dependent variable was delinquency as measured by the TOCA-R Aggressive/Disruption subscale. This scale is a teacher rating, which provides much richer data than simply relying on official data; however, it also only represents behavior in the classroom environment. The TOCA-R measures the social adaptational status and competency of the child at meeting the social task demands in the classroom, and the Aggression/Disruption subscale has been found to be highly reliable and a valid measure of delinquency in previous studies (Werthamer-Larsson, Kellam, & Wheeler, 1991; Rains, 2003; Schwartz, 1991) and in multiple research sites and studies (Johns Hopkins University Prevention Intervention Center First and Second Generation Trials in Chicago, IL and Baltimore, MD; Fast Track Project).

However, it sill has limitations as a measurement tool, especially in the middle and high school years. According to Life Course/Social Field Theory, the classroom is no longer the dominant social field in adolescence, a critical time period in the development of delinquency. The TOCA-R Aggression/Disruption scale is only intended to measure delinquency in the classroom and will therefore not include delinquency in other settings. The real limitation in the measurement would be in the middle and high schools when peer groups are the most dominant social field. This could result in the underestimation of delinquent behavior, and could explain why there is an early drop off of aggressive/disruptive behavior.

According to Moffitt, life-course-persistent offenders should be delinquent across time and environment, so they should be able to be identified using teacher ratings of delinquency. Adolescence-limited offenders, on the other hand, are highly influenced by their environments and offend to gain social recognition, which may not occur in the classroom. It should be more difficult to differentiate the adolescence-limited offenders and abstainers using teacher ratings since teachers are no longer the natural raters during adolescence. Research supports this hypothesis, as different latent factors have been found to underlie childhood and adolescent antisocial behavior (Bartusch, Lynam, Moffitt, & Silva, 1997). However, teacher ratings of antisocial behavior have been used for many of the previous group-based trajectory studies, and thus, makes this study comparable (e.g., Broidy et al., 2003).

One principal advantage in the measurement in this study is the availability of so many theoretically important constructs for Moffitt's taxonomy. There are measures of the subjects' psycho-physiological deviance and family dysfunction in childhood, which are central to her hypotheses about life-course-persistent offenders. Measures of deviant peers and environment are also available during adolescence, which is when Moffitt hypothesized that they are important factors in adolescence-limited offending. Finally, this study includes a proxy measure of social bonding, and how important friendship is, which could be associated with abstaining from delinquent behavior. With the availability of these variables, her hypotheses about the etiology of different trajectories can be empirically tested.

In respect to assessing Moffitt's theory, there are several measures that are not available for this dataset that are essential for testing her hypotheses. The most important measure that is not obtainable is a representation of the "maturity gap", or a discrepancy between physical and social maturity, which makes it impossible to test this very central feature of her theory. Other important measures that would have been helpful to have included are childhood medical problems and psychiatric diagnoses for the life-course-persistent group, and indicators of social status for the abstainers and adolescence-limited groups.

Statistical

The final category of limitations is statistical in nature. Group-based trajectory modeling in general, and general growth mixture modeling in particular, is a relatively new techniques. Using this method provides several challenges, ranging from the lack of established best practices to the uncertainty of the validity of its findings.

One of the greatest challenges with group-based trajectory modeling is the difficulty in finding an agreed upon and accepted methodology for model selection. There is a large number of criteria on which to base model selection, and researchers have yet to settle on a best practice. This study followed Nylund's (2007) recommendations for selecting a model, which included examining fit statistics, model parsimony, estimation problems (such as model non-convergence, negative variances, model non-identification, etc.), meaningfulness of class prevalence, level of discrimination between classes (entropy), and the theoretical fit of trajectories. Even with all of these conditions, there is still a possibility for researcher bias to be introduced during model selection.

Another methodological issue which has yet to be addressed in the literature, with the exception of (Kreuter & Muthen, 2007; 2008) is in the model specifications. With the advancement in modeling theory and statistical software, it is now possible to allow the separate estimation of within and between variance in the latent growth terms. Models can now be far more sophisticated, which brings up the question as to whether the methodology is currently more advanced and developed than the theories and if it is appropriate to use such a complex model. The flexibility provided in the estimation technique can be a double edged sword; while it allows a wide variety of procedures to test hypotheses, it is also very easy to overfit a model. This study took an empirical approach to advance current understanding of group-based trajectories and different variance structures of the latent growth terms as well as how model restrictions impact group means and variances, class proportions, and trajectory shapes were explored.

In addition to this problem, the classification of individuals into groups will never be perfect and should not be thought of as a method to place actual subjects into a group. The methodology is limited because it summarizes behavior and characteristics of individuals following similar developmental courses and individuals in each group do not necessarily follow the overall trajectory. Trajectory classes are clusters of individuals following approximately the same developmental course which has distinctive characteristics from other clusters. This can be challenging because of the understanding of group membership. Researchers have warned that the greatest danger in group-based trajectory modeling is in incorrect interpretation (Nagin, 2005). It is extremely important to interpret the results with caution and not to assign individuals to groups and to label them. This study used posterior class-membership profiles to identify and describe group characteristics in order to avoid this pitfall, but it is still an important issue to consider when considering and interpreting results from these types of models.

CONCLUSIONS

This study found partial support for Moffitt's developmental taxonomy. A three group model of delinquency was uncovered, but the three groups did not correspond entirely to her predictions. The data found two groups that matched her predictions, the abstainers and the adolescence-limited offenders (although there is no available data into adulthood to conclude that they desist from offending after adolescence). The third group does not match Moffitt's hypotheses, as they displayed high levels of delinquency in childhood and then declined through adolescence instead of displaying high levels throughout. Several of the predictors that Moffitt offered were found to be related to group membership, such as higher levels of hyperactivity and concentration problems in childhood in the more delinquent groups, deviant peer role models in the adolescence-limited group, and a strong belief in friendship in the abstainer group. Several of the other predictors that she offers in her theory were not related to delinquency trajectories. Overall, the results were mixed with respect to testing her taxonomy.

Methodological Conclusions

The first part of the study was conclusive. It found strong evidence that group-based trajectory modeling outperformed the standard growth modeling when examining delinquency measures over time. This empirically confirmed the idea of group classification and that there are distinct clusters of individuals that can be identified within a population who exhibit similar trajectories that are dissimilar to other clusters. This lends support for the idea of developmental taxonomies and that there are true subgroups of individuals and delinquent trajectories. This is important because there has been heavy debate even within developmental theorists of crime as to whether there are subgroups, or there are simply external covariates that determine the shape of trajectories over time (Sampson & Laub, 2005a). This study provides evidence that there are distinct groups and taxonomic theories are an appropriate and potentially useful approach for developmental theorists. Of course, it is still possible that these groupings are merely artifacts of mixtures of irregular but homogenous populations of repeated measures; however, with studies consistently finding similar trajectory classes, it is less likely.

Once it was found to be a superior method for capturing the growth process in delinquency, different model specifications were explored. The different latent variance structures had an impact on group enumeration, trajectory group membership, class proportions, and trajectory shape. Almost all of the previous studies using group-based trajectory modeling in the criminal justice literature restrict the variance factors to zero, which simplifies the parameterization of the model, but is also based on a theory that group membership is only meaningful if it is conceptualized as strictly as possible. This study found that loosening variance restrictions both improved the model fit empirically, but also made the most sense theoretically.

Using Moffitt's theory as a guide, the variance restrictions were removed one by one to establish which model specifications would be most meaningful both empirically and theoretically. The most widely used method in criminology was not the ideal approach to test Moffitt's theory in particular. It was concluded that using the least restrictive model both fit the data and the theory, and that the variance structures do have a large impact on the model and are worth further assessment. The implication for future research is that different variance restrictions can produce different models that should be explored during model development and selection.

Changing the mathematical definitions of a group influenced how they can and are interpreted theoretically. When testing a criminological theory, it is important to consider how a group is defined – is it a group of people who develop in an identical manner (with only error accounting for their differences), or will group members develop in a similar manner, but differ along their own distribution? If the people in the groups vary from one another, would each group vary the same amount? These questions should be considered and an appropriate model should be specified to match the theory. Many developmental theories do not explicitly specify how a group is defined in respect to how heterogeneous the members are (e.g., Moffit, 1993; Patterson, 1996). This paper found that one group (who are analogous to Moffit's "abstainer group") is significantly less heterogeneous than the other groups when the within group variation was estimated separately, leading to the conclusion that estimating the variance independently is a worthwhile use of degrees of freedom.

One of the most striking findings was that the stability of class proportions and parameters across the models. While class enumeration was different when variation was not modeled, once it was held constant, there was considerable model agreement. The group membership, however, was not nearly as consistent across the models. While it appeared that the groups were not changing with the different variance restrictions, the individuals who made up those groups, or at least their probabilities of belonging to the groups, were different. The largest difference when the within group variation was restricted to be equal across classes (variance invariance). Perhaps more significantly, once variation was freely estimated, it became apparent that one group was much more homogeneous than the others, which has major theoretical implications.

A strong argument for not modeling variation within or between groups is that the models end up exceedingly complex. If a model without variation results in an almost statistically-equivalent as one with variation, it would make more sense to stick with the one without variation for simplicity's sake. However, it will, in many cases, require more trajectory groups, which may or may not provide additional validity (and could even reduce it). In this case, the model that is the most complex, the varying variance model, does produce a better model in respect to both the model fit statistics and measures of concurrent validity and the additional parameters were worth the loss of model parsimony.

Another interesting finding was the differences in suspension and substance use initiation rates by group in all the different models. It appears that none of the models predict these alternative measures of delinquency extremely accurately. Theoretically, a no variance model should produce groups that are the most homogeneous and would display the largest differential manifestations of other delinquency measures and patterns, but this was not the case. In fact, the more "homogenous" the groups were, the fewer differences in alternative measures of delinquency were observed. Requirements of homogeneity, both within and between classes, unexpectedly negatively impacted the concurrent validity. Overall, the three class varying variance model produced groups with the most distinguishable rates of suspension, and tobacco, marijuana, and illicit drug use initiation, which was unexpected as adding random effects should theoretically create groups that are more heterogeneous. Overall, the answer to whether the groups possess any external validity once they are defined more broadly was less clear. While the groups did manifest different substance use initiation and school suspension rates, the differences were not as large as would be anticipated by the theory. This calls into question the meaningfulness of group membership; however, the most important measure of group membership would be distal measures of criminality, which are not yet available. It is premature to draw conclusions about the external validity of group membership.

Allowing variation within and/or between groups also opens modeling opportunities that are not possible with the traditional models that do not specify variation. With these more complex models, differences within groups can be explored and modeled. The modeling opportunities are almost endless, which yet again emphasizes that the statistical methods currently available may be more advanced than the theories that are being tested. This studies demonstrated that statistical models can be very sophisticated which and presents the question as to whether the methodology is currently more advanced and developed than the theories it is testing.

Theoretical Conclusions

The next part of the study, a thorough examination of the trajectories in relation to Moffitt's theory, did not produce such clear-cut results. Her hypotheses about the correlates of group membership were somewhat confirmed. Consistent with her hypotheses, all of the predictors that were theoretically relevant performed better predicting group membership than either a general growth model or the within group variation in a group-based model. This provides additional concurrent validity to the distinct groupings and that they are not simply different parts of an underlying distribution (normal or otherwise).

While there were three groups, as anticipated by Moffitt, they did not fit her hypotheses about the size or the trajectory shape of the groups. Only one of the groups actually fit her model, which was the abstainer group. However, it was made up of a much larger proportion of the sample than she estimated. The second group, the adolescence-limited offenders, made up a much small proportion of the sample than expected, and did not peak in late adolescence. It is impossible to determine from the data available whether the adolescence-limited group will desist from delinquent behavior in adulthood, so the moniker of "adolescence-limited" may not be warranted. The final group, the life-course-persistent offenders, did not match her theory in respect to the shape of their trajectories. While they did begin first grade displaying much higher levels of aggression and disruption in the classroom, they desisted from this behavior throughout the study, until their group mean actually fell below the adolescence-limited offender group. Again, since this study only followed individuals until the end of high school, it is impossible to know whether the label "life-course-persistent" is appropriate because their offending patterns in adulthood have yet to be established.

As Moffitt predicted, hyperactivity and concentration problems in childhood were related to the highest trajectory group. On the other hand, these predictors also differentiated the adolescence-limited and abstainer group members, which conflicts with her theory. Congruent with her predictions, peer deviance in adolescence is related to the higher offending groups, and a strong belief in social bonds is related to abstaining from delinquency. However, contrary to her theory and findings from previous studies, the early measures of psychological and family dysfunction were not found to be related to any of the offending patterns. The largest risk factors uncovered in this analysis were both measures that are easy to collect from classroom a teacher, which makes them practical for purposes of identifying children who could benefit from additional services.

Next Steps

This study has raised many issues, both methodological and theoretical, that should be explored in future research. First of all, latent variance structures proved to be important model specifications that appreciably impacted the research findings. This issue has received very little attention in the criminological literature (with the exception of Kreuter & Muthen, 2008, who did not discuss the theoretical implications of changing model specifications) and should be considered in future for theory testing using group-based trajectory modeling. It would also be instructive to reconsider the major studies that used this methodology and re-estimate models with looser variance restrictions and find out if the groups change proportions, membership, and shape.

The measures used to model delinquency also need to be carefully considered when testing Moffitt's theory. In order to comprehensively test her theory, measures of delinquency should reflect multiple domains, especially in adolescence, to differentiate the three groups. In addition to modeling delinquency over multiple domains, the different natural raters in each domain at each life stage should be included in future research.

The follow-up period is also essential for testing this particular theory and should be extended into and through adulthood. As this sample ages, it will continue to be followed-up. Hopefully the data will be available to test these developmental trajectories and whether they are related to more distal criminological outcomes.

And finally, different predictors should be explored. One of the main elements of Moffitt's taxonomy is the "maturity gap" that motivates adolescence-limited offenders to engage in delinquency. Unfortunately there were no indicators of either physical or social maturity available for this sample to test this portion of her theory. Other important variables to consider in the future include more and/or alternate measures of environmental and psycho-physiological dysfunction in early childhood, deviant peer role models, perceived social status, and strong bonds to positive peers in adolescence.

Additional research is needed to better document, recognize, and understand how and why delinquency trajectories develop over time. If Moffitt's taxonomy and its predictors can be empirically validated, risk factors for life-course-persistent and adolescence-limited offending patterns can be identified. These factors can be used to identify children who are at high risk for different lifelong offending patterns for prevention and intervention programming. As the cost-effectiveness of prevention/intervention programming is largely dependent on the degree to which children can be recognized as more likely in engaging in antisocial behavior, the fact that teacher ratings are valid and relatively economical to obtain is encouraging. This study demonstrated that early concentration problems and hyperactivity are risk factors for higher delinquency trajectories, and may be useful in identifying and referring children for programs to help prevent the expression of these delinquent trajectories. Further studies should investigate other risk factors and whether it is possible to alter developmental trajectories through prevention or intervention programming.

References

Achenback, T.M. & Edelbrock, C. (1987). *Manual for the Youth Self-Report and Profile*. Burlington, VT: University of Vermont Department of Psychiatry.

Agnew, R. (1991). The interactive effects of peer variables on delinquency. *Criminology, 29(*1), 47-72.

Akaike, H. (1987). Factor analysis and AIC. *Psychometrika, 52*, 317-332.

Bartusch, D.R.J., Lynam, D.R., Moffitt, T.E., & Silva, P.A. (1997). Is age important? Testing a general versus developmental theory of antisocial behavior. *Criminology, 35*(1), 13-48.

Bauer, D.J., & Curran, P.J. (2003). Distributional assumptions of growth mixture models: Implications for overextraction of latent trajectory classes. *Psychological Methods, 8*(3), 338-363.

Bauer, D.J., & Curran, P.J. (2004). The integration of continuous and discrete latent variable models: Potential problems and promising opportunities. *Psychological Methods, 9*(1), 3-29.

Bentler, P.M. (1988). Comparative fit indexes in structural models. *Psychological Bulletin, 107*, 238-246.

Block, J. H. (1971). *Mastery learning: Theory and practice*. New York: Holt, Rinehart & Winston.

Blockland, A.A., Nagin, D.S., & Nieuwbeerta, P. (2005). Life span offending trajectories of a Dutch conviction cohort. *Criminology, 43*(4), 919-954.

Blumstein, A., & Cohen, J. (1987). Characterizing criminal careers. *Science, 237*, 985-991.

Blumstein, A., Cohen, J., & Farrington, D. (1988). Criminal career research: Its value for criminology. *Criminology, 26*, 1-35.

Bongers, I.L., Koot, H.M., van der Ende, J., & Verhulst, F.C. (2004). Developmental trajectories of externalizing behaviors in childhood and adolescence. *Child Development, 75*, 1523-1537.

Brame, R., Mulvey, E., & Piquero, A. (2001). On the development of different kinds of criminal activity. *Sociological Methods and Research, 29*, 319-341.

Brame, R., Nagin, D.S., & Tremblay, R.E. (2001). Developmental trajectories of physical aggression from school entry to late adolescence. *Journal of Child Psychology and Psychiatry, 42*, 503-512.

Broidy L.M., Nagin, D.S., Tremblay, R.E., Bates, J.E., Brame, R., Dodge, K.A., Fergusson, D.M., Horwood, J.L., Laird, R., Lynam, D.R., Moffitt, T.E., Petit, G.S., & Vitaro, F. (2003). Developmental trajectories of childhood disruptive behaviors and adolescent delinquency: A six-site, cross-national study. *Developmental Psychology, 39*, 222-245.

Browne, M.W., & Cudeck, R. (1993). Alternative ways of assessing model fit. In K.A. Bollen and J.S. Long (Eds.), *Testing Structural Models*. Newbury Park: Sage Publications.

Bushway, S.D., Brame, R., & Paternoster, R. (1999). Assessing stability and change in criminal offending: A comparison of random effects, semiparametric, and fixed effects modeling strategies. *Journal of Quantitative Criminology, 15*(2), 129-153.

Bushway, S.D., Piquero, A.R., Broidy, L.M., Cauffman, E., & Mazerolle, P. (2001). An empirical freamework for studying desistance as a process. *Criminology, 39*(2), 491-516.

Bushway, S.D., Thornberry, T., & Krohn, M.D. (2003). Desistence as a developmental process: A comparison of static and dynamic approaches. *Journal of Quantitative Criminology, 19*: 289-297.

Capaldi, D.M, & Patterson, G.R. (1989). *Psychometric properties of fourteen latent constructs from the Oregon Youth Study*. New York City: Springer-Verlag.

Caspi, A., & Moffitt, T.E. (1991). Individual differences are accentuated during periods of social change: The sample case of girls at puberty. *Journal of Personality and Social Psychology, 61*(1), 157-168.

Chung, I.J., Hill, K.G., Hawking, D., Gilchrist, L.D. (2002). Childhood predictors of offense trajectories. *Journal of Research in Crime and Delinquency, 39*, 60-90.

D'Unger, A.V., Land, K.C., & McCall, P.L. (2002). Sex differences in age patterns of delinquent/criminal careers: Results from Poisson Latent Class Analyses of the Philadelphia Birth Cohort. *Journal of Quantitative Criminology, 18*(4), 349-375.

D'Unger, A.V., Land, K.C., McCall, P.L., & Nagin, D.S. (1998). How many latent classes of delinquent/criminal careers? Results from Mixed Poisson Regression Analysis of the London, Philadelphia, and Racine Cohort Studies. *American Journal of Sociology, 103*, 1593-1630.

Eggleston, E.P, Laub, J.H., & Sampson, R.J. (2004). Methodological sensitivities to latent class analysis of long-term criminal trajectories. *Journal of Quantitative Criminology, 20*(1), 1-26.

Elliott, D.S., Ageton, S.S., Huizinga, D., Knowles, B.A., & Canter, R.J. (1983). *The prevalence and incidence of delinquent behavior: 1976-1980.* (The National Youth Survey Report No. 26). Boulder, CO: Behavioral Research Institute.

Elliott, D.S., Huizinga, D, & Ageton, S.S. (1985). *Explaining delinquency and drug use.* Beverly Hills, CA: Sage Publications.

Farrington, D.P. (1986). Age and crime. In M. Tonry & N. Morris (Eds.), *Crime and Justice: An Annual Review of Research* (Vol. 7, pp. 189-250). Chicago: University of Chicago Press.

Farrington, D., Ohlin, L., & Wilson, J.Q. (1986). *Understanding and controlling crime: Toward a new research strategy.* Report commissioned by the MacArthur Foundation, Chicago, IL. New York: Springer-Violag.

Felson, R.B., & Haynie, D.L. (2002). Pubertal development, social factors, and delinquency among adolescent boys. *Criminology, 40*(4), 967 – 988.

Fergusson, D.M., & Horwood, L.J. (2002). Male and female offending trajectories. *Development and Psychopathology, 14,* 159-177.

Francis, B., Soothill, K., & Fligelstone, R. (2004). Identifying patterns and pathways of offending behaviour: A new approach to typologies of crime. *European Journal of Criminology, 1,* 47-88.

Furr-Holden, D.D., Ialongo, N.S., Anthony, J.C., Petras, H., & Kellam, S. (2004). Developmentally inspired drug prevention: Middle school outcomes in a school-based randomized prevention trail. *American Journal of Community Psychology, 27*(5), 599-641.

Fuzhong, L., Duncan, T.E., Duncan, S.C., & Acock, A. (2001). Latent growth modeling of longitudinal data: A finite growth mixture modeling approach. *Structural Equation Modeling, 8*(4), 493-530.

Gottfredson, M.R., & Hirschi, T. (1990). *A general theory of crime.* Standford, CA: Stanford University Press.

Hawkins, J.D., Catalano, R.F., & Miller, J.Y. (1998). Risk and protective factors for alcohol and other drug problems in adolescence and early adulthood: Implications for substance abuse prevention. *Psychological Bulletin, 112*(11), 64-105.

Herrenkohl, T.I., Maguin, E., Hill, K.G., Hawking, J.D., Abbott, R.D., & Catalano, R.F. (2000). Developmental risk factors for youth violence. *Journal of Adolescent Health, 26,* 176-186.

Hirschi, T. (1969). *Causes of delinquency*. Los Angeles: University of Los Angeles Press.

Hirschi, T., & Gottfredson, M. (1985). Age and crime, logic and scholarship: Comment on Greenberg. *American Journal of Sociology, 91*, 22-27.

Ialongo, N.S., Kellam, S.G., & Poduska, J. (1999). *Manual for Baltimore How I Feel (Technical Report Number 2)*. Baltimore, MD: Johns Hopkins University.

Ialongo, N.S., Werthamer, L., Kellam, S.G., Brown, C.H., Wang, S., & Lin, Y. (1999). Proximal impact of two first-grade preventive interventions on the early risk behaviors for later substance abuse, depression, and antisocial behavior. *Drug and Alcohol Dependence, 66*(1), 51-60.

Jones, R. & Nagin, D.S. (2005). *Advances in group-based trajectory modeling and a SAS procedure for estimating them*. Working Paper, Carnegie Mellon University.

Jones, R., Nagin, D.S., & Roeder, K. (2001). A SAS procedure based on mixture models for estimating developmental trajectories. *Sociological Research and Methods, 29*, 374-93.

Kellam, S.G., Rebok, G.W., Ialongo, N., & Mayer, L.S. (1994). The course and malleability of aggressive behavior from early first grade into middle school: Results of a developmental epidemiologically-based preventive trial. *Journal of Child Psychological, Psychiatry, and Allied Disciplines, 35*, 259-281.

Kratzer, L, & Hodgins, S. (1999). A typology of offenders: A test of Moffitt's theory among males and females from childhood to age 30. *Criminal Behavior and Mental Health, 9*(1), 57-73.

Kreuter, F. & Muthén, B. (2007). Longitudinal modeling of population heterogeneity: Methodological challenges to the analysis of empirically derived criminal trajectory profiles. G.R. Hancock., and K.M Samuelsen, K. M. (eds.), *Advances in latent variable mixture models*, Information Age Publishing, Inc., Charlotte, NC.

Kreuter, F. & Muthén, B. (2008). Analyzing criminal trajectory profiles: Bridging multilevel and group-based approaches using growth mixture modeling. *Journal of Quantitative Criminology, 24:* 1-31.

Lambert, S.F., Ialongo, N.S., Boyd, R.C., & Cooley, M.R. (2005). Risk factors for community violence exposure in adolescence. *American Journal of Community Psychology, 36*, 29-48.

Lancourse, E., Nagin, D., Vitaro, F., Claes, M., & Tremblay, R. (2003). Developmental trajectories of boys' delinquent group membership and facilitation of violent behaviors during adolescence. *Developmental and Psychopathology, 15,* 228-240.

Laub, J.H, Nagin, D.S., & Sampson, R.J. (1998). Trajectories of change in criminal offending: Good marriages and the desistance process. *American Sociological Review, 63,* 225-238.

Lo, Y., Mendell, N.R., & Rubin, D.B. (2001). Testing the number of components in a normal mixture. *Biometrika, 88*(3), 767-778.

Loeber, R. (1982). The stability of antisocial and delinquent child behavior: A review. *Child Development, 53,* 1431-1446.

Loeber, R., Stouthamer-Loeber, M., Van Kammen, W., & Farrington, D.P. (1989). Development of a new measure of self-reported antisocial behavior for young children: Prevalence and reliability. In M. Klein (Ed.), *Cross-national research in self-reported crime and delinquency* (pp. 203-226). Boston: Kluwer-Nijhoff.

Maughan, B., Pickles, A., Rowe, R., Costello, E.J., & Angold, A. (2000). Developmental trajectories of aggressive and non-aggressive conduct problems. *Journal of Quantitative Criminology, 16*(2), 199-221.

McLachlan, G., & Peel, D. (2000). *Finite mixture models.* New York: JohnWiley & Sons.

Mears, D.P., Ploeger, M., & Warr, M. (1988). Explaining the gender gap in delinquency: Peer influence and moral evaluations of behavior. *Journal of Research in Crime and Delinquency, 35*(3), 251-266.

Mischel, L, & Roy, J. (2006). *Rethinking high school graduation rates and trends.* Washingtin, D.C.: Economic Policy Institute.

Moffitt, T.E. (1990). Juvenile delinquency and attention deficit disorder: Boys' developmental trajectories from age 3 to age 15. *Child Development, 61,* 893-910.

Moffitt, T.E. (1993). Adolescence-limited and life-course-persistent antisocial behavior: A developmental taxonomy. *Psychological Review, 100*(4), 674-701.

Moffitt, T.E. (1994). National histories of delinquency. In E.G.M. Weitekamp and J. Kerner (Eds.), *Cross-national longitudinal research on human development and criminal behavior.* Dordrecht, Netherlands: Kluwer Academic.

Moffitt, T.E. (1997). Adolescence-limited and life-course-persistent offending: A complementary pair of developmental theories. In

T.P. Thornberry (Ed.), *Developmental theories of crime and delinquency, advances in criminological theory, vol. 7.* New Brunswick, NJ: Transaction Publishers.

Moffitt, T.E. (2006). Life-course persistent verses adolescence-limited antisocial behavior. In Dante Cicchetti & D. Cohen (Eds.), *Developmental Psychopathology, 2nd Edition.* New York: Wiley.

Moffitt, T. E., Lynam, D. R., & Silva, P. A. (1994). Neuropsychological tests predicting persistent male delinquency. *Criminology, 32,* 277-300.

Moffitt, T.E., & Silva, P.A. (1988). IQ and delinquency: A direct test of the differential hypothesis. *Journal of Abnormal Psychology, 97,* 330-333.

Muthén, B. (1989). Latent variables modeling in heterogeneous populations. *Psychometrika, 54,* 557-585.

Muthén, B. (2000). Methodological issues in random coefficient growth modeling using a latent variable framework: Applications to the development of heavy drinking in ages 18–37. In J. S. Rose, L. Chassin, C. Presson, & J. Sherman (Eds.), *Multivariate applications in substance use research: New methods for new questions* (pp. 113–140). Mahwah, NJ: Erlbaum.

Muthén, B. (2004). Latent variable analysis. In D. Kaplan (Ed.), *The Sage handbook of quantitative methodology for the social sciences.* New York: Sage.

Muthén, B., Brown, C.H., Masyn, K., Jo, B., Khoo, S., Yang, C., Wang, C., Kellam, S., Carlin, J., & Liao, J. (2002). General growth mixture modeling for randomized preventive interventions. *Biostatistics, 3*(4), 459-475.

Muthén, B., & Muthén, L. (1998-2004). *Mplus user's guide. 3rd Edition.* Los Angeles: Muthén & Muthén.

Nagin, D.S. (2005). *Group-based modeling of development.* Cambridge, MA: University Press.

Nagin, D.S., Farrington, D., & Moffitt, T. (1995). Life-course trajectories of different types of offenders. *Criminology, 33,* 111-139.

Nagin, D. S., & Land, K.C. (1993). Age, criminal careers, and population heterogeneity: Specification and estimation of a nonparametric, Mixed Poisson Model." *Criminology 31,* 327-362

Nagin, D.S., Pagani, L., Tremblay, R., & Vitaro, F. (2003). Life course turning points: A case study of the effects of school failure on interpersonal violence. *Development and Psychopathology, 15,* 343-361.

Nagin, D.S., & Tremblay, R.E. (1999). Trajectories of boys' physical aggression, opposition, and hyperactivity on the path to physically violent and nonviolent juvenile delinquency. *Child Developmental, 70,* 1181-1196.

Nagin, D.S., & Tremblay, R.E. (2001a). Parental and early childhood predictors of persistent physical aggression in boys from kindergarten to high school. *Archives of General Psychiatry, 50,* 389-394.

Nagin, D.S., & Tremblay, R.E. (2001b). Analyzing developmental trajectories of distinct but related behaviors: A group-based method. *Psychological Methods, 6,* 18-34.

Nagin, D.S., & Tremblay, R.E. (2004). *Developmental trajectory groups: Fact or fiction?* Unpublished manuscript.

Nagin, D.S., & Tremblay, R.E. (2005a). What has been learned from group-based trajectory modeling? Examples from physical aggression and other problem behaviors. *Annals, AAPSS, 602,* 82-117.

Nagin, D.S. & Tremblay, R.E. (2005b). Developmental trajectory groups: Fact or a useful statistical fiction? *Criminology, 43*(4), 873-904.

Nebesio, T., & Pescoritz, O.H. (2005). Historical perspectives: Endocrine disruptions and the timing of puberty. *The Endocrinologist, 15*(1), 44-48.

Nylund, K. L., Asparouhov. A., & Muthén, B. (2006). Deciding on the number of classes in latent class analysis and growth mixture modeling. A Monte Carlo study, submitted for publication.

Patternoster, R., Brame, R., & Farrington, D.P. (2001). One the relationship between adolescent and adult conviction frequencies. *Journal of Quantitative Criminology, 17,* 201-226.

Patterson, G. R. (1996). Some characteristics of a developmental theory for early-onset delinquency. In M.F. Lenzenweger & J.J. Haugaard (Eds.) *Frontiers of developmental psychopathology.* New York: Oxford University Press.

Piquero, A.R. (2005). *Taking stock of developmental trajectories of criminal activity over the lifecourse.* Paper presented at the National Institutes of Justice, Washington, D.C.

Piquero, A.R., Blumstein, A., Brame, R., Haapenen, R., Mulvey, E.P., & Nagin, D.S. (2001). Assessing the impact of exposure time and incapacitation on longitudinal trajectories of criminal offending. *Journal of Adolescent Research, 16,* 54-74.

Piquero, A.R., Brame, R., Mazerolle, P., & Haapanen, R. (2002). Crime in emerging adulthood. *Criminology, 40,* 137-169.

Piquero, A.R., Brezina, T., & Turner, M.G. (2005). Testing Moffitt's account of delinquency abstention. *Journal of Research in Crime and Delinquency, 42*(1), 27-54.

Raine, A., Loeber, R., Stouthamer-Loeber, M., Moffitt, T.E., Caspi, A., & Lynam, D. (2005). Neurocognitive impairments in boys on the life-course-persistent antisocial path. *Journal of Abnormal Psychology, 114*(1), 38-49.

Rains, C. (2003). *Teacher Observation of Child Adaptation-Revised (TOCA-R)* (Fast TrackProject Technical Report). Available from the Fast Track Project website: http://www.fasttrackproject.org.

Raudenbush, S.W. (2005). How do we study "What happens next"? *Annals, AAPSS, 602,* 131-144.

Raudenbush, S.W., & Bryk, A.S. (2002). *Hierarchical linear models: Applications and data analysis methods, second edition.* Thousand Oaks, CA: Sage Publications.

Robins, L. (1966), *Deviant children grown up.* Baltimore: Williams and Wilkins.

Robins, L. (1978). Sturdy childhood predictors of adult antisocial behavior: Replication from longitudinal studies. *Psychological Medicine, 8,* 611-622.

Rutter, M., Giller, H., & Hagell, A. (1998). *Antisocial behavior by young people.* Cambridge: Cambridge University Press. Sampson, R.J., & Laub, J.H. (1992). Crime and deviance in the life course. *Annual Review of Sociology, 18,* 63-84.

Sampson, R.J., & Laub, J.H. (1993). *Crime in the making.* Cambridge, MA: Harvard University Press.

Sampson, R.J., & Laub, J.H. (2003). Life-course desisters? Trajectories of crime among delinquent boys followed to age 70. *Criminology, 41,* 555-592.

Sampson, R.J., & Laub, J.H. (2005a). A life-course view of the development of crime. *Annals, AAPSS, 602,* 12-45.

Sampson, R.J., & Laub, J.H. (2005b). Seductions of method: Rejoinder to Nagin and Tremblay's "Developmental trajectory groups: Fact or fiction?" *Criminology, 43*(4), 905-914.

Sampson, R. J., Laub, J.H.,& Eggleston, E.P. (2004). On the robustness and validity of groups. *Journal of Quantitative Criminology, 20*(1), 37-42

Schaeffer, C.M., Petras, H., Ialongo, N., Poduska, J., & Kellam, S. (2003). Modeling growth in boys' aggressive behavior across elementary school: links to later criminal involvement, conduct disorder, and antisocial personality disorder. *Developmental Psychology, 39*(6), 1020-1025.

Schwartz, D. (1991). *TOCA Summary Report* (Fast Track Project Technical Report). Nashville, TN: Vanderbilt University, Fast Track Project.

Shaw, D.S., Gilliom, M., Ingoldsby, E.M., & Nagin, D.S. (2003). Trajectories leading to school-age conduct problems. *Developmental Psychology, 39*, 189-200.

Shaw, D.S., Lacourse, E., & Nagin, D.S. (2005). Developmental trajectories of conduct problems and hyperactivity from ages 2 to 10. *Journal of Child Psychology and Psychiatry, 49*(9), 931-942.

Storr, C.L., Ialongo, N.S., Kellam, S.G., & Anthony, J.C. (2002). A randomized controlled trial of two primary school intervention strategies to prevent early onset tobacco smoking. *Drug and Alcohol Dependence, 73*(2), 149-158.

Tremblay, R.E., Nagin, D., Seguin, J., Zoccolillo, M., Zelazo, P., Boivin, M., Perusse, D., & Japel, C. (2004). Physical aggression during early childhood: Trajectories and predictors. *Pediatrics, 114*, 43-50.

Van Lier, P.A., Muthén, B.O., van der Sar, R.M., & Crijnen, A.A. (2004). Preventing disruptive behavior in elementary schoolchildren: Impact of a universal classroom-based intervention. *Journal of Consulting and Clinical Psychology, 72*(3), 467-478.

Weakliem, D.L. (1999). A critique of Bayesian Information Criterion for model selection. *Sociological Methods and Research, 27*(3), 359-197.

Weitekamp, E.G.M., & Kerner, H.J. (1994). *Cross-national longitudinal research on human development and criminal behavior.* Dordrecht, Netherlands: Kluwer Academic Publishers.

Werthamer-Larsson, L., Kellam, S.G., & Wheeler, L., (1991). Effects of first-grade classroom environment on child shy behavior, aggressive behavior, and concentration problems. *American Journal of Community Psychology, 19*, 585-602.

White, H.R., Bates, M.E., & Buyske, S. (2001). Adolescence-limited verses persistent delinquency: Extending Moffitt's hypothesis into adulthood. *Journal of Abnormal Psychology, 110,* 600-609.

Index